TO LOVE IS TO OBEY

TO LOVE IS TO OBEY

Living the Commands of Jesus

by

Guthrie E. Janssen

HOLY CROSS ORTHODOX PRESS
Brookline, Massachusetts 02146

©1986 by Holy Cross Orthodox Press
Published by Holy Cross Orthodox Press
50 Goddard Avenue
Brookline, Masachusetts 02146

Cover design by Mary C. Vaporis

Library of Congress Cataloging-in-Publication Data

Janssen, Guthrie E.
To love is to obey.

1. Christian life – Orthodox Eastern authors. 2. Love – Religious
aspects – Christianity. I. Title.
BX382.J36   248.4'819   87-4045
ISBN 0-917651-38-3

For Alfred and Frances

CONTENTS

Eastern Christianity, which remains faithful to an earlier Christian tradition, may again invigorate the West.

Robert Payne

. . .the Eastern Church represents something which we have lost. . . . We should not imagine that we have nothing to learn from them. It may happen that with centuries of more intimate contact, the dimension of depth may again enter Western thinking.

Paul Tillich

Chapter One

THE WAY OF LIFE

I want to begin by speaking about a donkey. That may seem a strange way to begin a book about love, but the reasons will become apparent.

I lived for many years in Egypt, where donkeys are common. One day, standing at the window of my room at The American University in Cairo I watched a small two-wheeled flatbed cart going past, with about ten peasant women crowded onto it and a man up front holding the reins of a small donkey that was pulling the cart. Just as they passed me, the weight became too much for the donkey and he went down, his four legs splayed flat on the pavement in all four directions. The women screamed and jumped off, and the man took a whip and began beating the donkey. The donkey got up, the women and the man climbed back onto the cart and the donkey staggered on with his load until he probably fell again somewhere farther on.

The point is that the donkey is not an esteemed animal in the Middle East, nor ever has been. Neither noble nor beautiful, it is treated with contempt, serviceable beast though it is. Even in this country donkeys are not highly regarded. Go into a bar or a truck stop anywhere and call someone a donkey and you're likely to come out with a broken jaw.

So why are we speaking about donkeys? Read Matthew 21.1-9, or Mark 11.1-10, or Luke 19.29-38. *The donkey is the throne of God!* We will return to this a number of times and will begin to realize its lesson for us in how to live a Christian life.

* * * * *

We turn now to another story[1] that is so familiar as to have almost lost all significance for us. We perceive it as "just a story" rather than *an experienced reality*. Yet together with the story of Jesus, the incarnation of God, it is one of the two most important accounts of human experience in all history. It is the story of Adam and Eve. Let us see it afresh. If we will do that, we will see ourselves and some terribly important facts about ourselves.

God created Adam, as we know, and gave him life (Genesis 2.7); and he placed Adam in a garden and gave him a job (Genesis 2.15). Then God put Adam to sleep and from him created Eve (Genesis 2.21-22).

Adam woke up. Beside him was the most gorgeous creature he had ever seen. Adam, remember, had already seen all the animals and birds and named them (Genesis 2.19). This was something else. Adam was moved. He was seeing glory incarnate. Adam was in love, and being in love he was also *in God*, and God in him (we will explain this more later on). Adam, however, remembered that God, who created him, was the primary glory and that Eve was therefore but a reflection, a created glory. Eve also looked upon Adam, and *she* fell in love. Domestic life began.

One day Eve wandered off into the woods and encountered a terribly handsome creature called the serpent (it was not until afterward that God condemned the serpent to crawl on his belly in dust and ugliness – Genesis 3.14). He told her a lie, and she bought it. (How could so beautiful a creature tell a lie? Passion stirred in her.) She then "sold" the lie to Adam, whose subsequent behavior was far worse than hers, as we shall see. Thus the "fall." All this is familiar, except for the depths of its implications.

So Adam and Eve when they heard the sound of God in the Garden hid themselves – hid from love, which is God (1 John 4.8) – and the first thing Adam said was, "I was afraid" (Genesis 3.10). For disobedience had set up a hostility to love, and the result was fear. An antinomy, a contradiction of spirit had invaded the harmony of the garden. This could not be tolerated. Adam and Eve had to go.

What we will describe now is not in scripture but part of the human record since the "fall":

Once out of the garden, Adam was aware that he was now unemployed. He had not lost the talent for agriculture that God had given him when he commanded him to keep the garden, but he was on his own. His fear remained. God was gone (or so it seemed to Adam, though God was nearby, desiring to receive his repentance). But Adam was trying to live by a certain stubborn pride, still in a spirit of self-assertive disobedience. He looked at Eve in a false awareness that she had caused all this, and he loathed her. She was only human after all, and he slapped her. She cringed, and he felt horrible. Suddenly he saw the glorious creature who had lain beside him, and God was gone, so he decided to worship *her*. He made her his goddess.

It didn't work. She was human, and she had sinned and had lost love, as had Adam. She was not God, however much of his glory she might retain. Adam perceived that his salvation (if he was to have any – he wasn't sure) lay in work. Adam became a workaholic. He would *work* his way back to Eden – or in his own strength build a new Eden. That didn't work either.

One day Adam chanced to eat an herb that in a few moments sent him off into pink clouds of rapturous escape, and he felt he had stumbled on the road back to Eden. It was at least an escape from the intolerable present. Eve saw it all and screamed, "Stop it!" And he left her.

When he had sobered up he returned. Now guilt weighed upon him. Adam began to live a life of quiet desperation. Eve decided that what worked was to be shrill, and she remained so. She also decided she would from now on wear the pants in the family. Resentful of this, Adam took on an attitude of superiority. Meanwhile, the children, sensing the ambient anger all around them, were distressed, especially Cain. Silently in his heart he determined to take revenge on someone one day.

With Adam and Eve's disobedience to God, a spirit of opposition now permeated their lives, for God is *he who is* (Exodus 3.14); there is no other, so to disobey him is to oppose him and to *live a lie*. Thus deceit had entered, and to hide their deceit, each began to construct a personal facade. Now the lie was all about them and in them. The good that God had created was gravely distorted. They now knew good *and* evil. Contradiction and opposition became their daily lot, and with these, enmities, and gradually Adam discovered that his own worst enemy was himself.

Do we begin to get the picture? There is no need to go farther. This is the human predicament. A frightful game is being played out by autonomous persons, each claiming self-assertive "rights," when God meant for them to have unity with one another *in him*. The implications of this are glaringly apparent in all human history. We see our own selves here. *Adam and Eve are us.* They did not see, as we can see because God himself has shown us in his son, that the recovery of Eden and of unity and joy and fearlessness must be by our becoming obedient again. It is only through restoration of obedience that we will find love, which is God, without whom we cannot live. Not only that, but God so loves us even in our disobedience that after we again become obedient to him he does far more that return us to Eden; *he gives us heaven itself, where we are to rule together with his own beloved Son* (Revelation 3.21)!

Restoration of the Unity

This is a book therefore about the restoration of our unity with God, our "rebirth" into his kingdom (John 3:3) through love and obedience.

This will not, however, be a manual of techniques. The restoration is accomplished through our gaining wisdom and understanding. We will discover that love is bound up with wisdom, and that wisdom is union with God. If we desire to have love – to be loved, to give love, to have the joy of love – the path to it is the way of wisdom. To follow this path is not just an intellectual exercise. It is something we *do* with all our being.

The "doing" consists of quietly, steadily, day in and day out, moment by moment obeying God in undemanding humility. The way of wisdom and understanding which leads to love is the way of obedience to him who made us, and we will discover that it is the way of living the fullest and richest possible life. This is not, however, the obedience of slaves, of mindless subordination, but an informed obedience that springs from knowledge of the truth about God and about our own desperate condition. Our obedience is to the commands of Jesus Christ, who is the embodiment of love and truth (John 14.6), and whose commands have absolute authority because he is the Son of God and all the authority of God the Father is in him (Matthew 28.18; John 5.17-47). None of this is beyond our capability, for God created every man (and woman), educated or not, with the capacity for knowledge and understanding, wisdom and love, and Christ commands of us nothing that we cannot accomplish, for he gives us the grace to do what he commands.

There is a brief statement which sums up all that we are trying to say here. It is in fact a summary of what the Christian faith is all about. It occurs at the beginning of a very ancient work attributed to the Apostles, called the *The Didache* (di-tha-he'), which is Greek for "the teaching." It reads:

There are two Ways: a Way of Life and a Way of Death, and the difference between these two Ways is great.

The Way of Life is this: Thou shalt love first the Lord thy Creator, and secondly thy neighbor as thyself . . .

This brings us to a revelation about ourselves that may be shocking when we reflect on it. Most of us assume that as Christians we have of course chosen the Way of Life. But has the reality struck us that whether we follow Jesus Christ and obey what he has commanded us is literally a life and death matter? Probably for most of us it has not. We are not accustomed to thinking about spiritual matters in such a radical way. Most of us tend to be lukewarm about our faith, and what happens to lukewarm Christians we will discover at the end of this book.

Our purpose in the meantime is to seek the Way of Love and learn how to follow it. Jesus left us specific commands to direct us in that way. (The earliest Christians, we may remember, were called "the people of the way" even before they were called Christians.) We will review most of those commands, bringing to bear understandings from many sources. We will be referring especially to the teachers of the first 1,000 years of the Church, who had profound insights, and to the understandings of Eastern Orthodoxy, which adheres to early traditions of the Church and can teach us much that we here in the West have lost. This is going to take us into some deep waters, but they will not be over our heads. The reason they are deep is because of the enormity of our alienation from God. The magnitude of our alienation is the negative correlation of the magnitude of God's love for us, which is inestimably great. In the eyes of the early teachers of the Church and of Orthodoxy today, our predicament is not attributable to this or that sin, horrendous though some of them are. God is not a terrorist trying to frighten us into doing what he wants. Rather, he sees that we exist in utter darkness and the dungeon of death until we receive the light of Christ (Isaiah 42.7). He desires us to surrender our total being to him, so that he may give us life.

The Clouding of Western Understanding

Once we decide to receive the light of Christ and to follow wherever it leads, we are confronted with severe obstacles. This is especially true for us in the United States, where life up to now has been relatively good and comfortable. People who have repeatedly suffered devastations are the ones who realize there is something radically wrong with the human situation that only God can cure. Here are some of the stumbling blocks we find in the culture that surrounds us:

1. Obedience is not popular with us. More often than not it is ridiculed. More important, we are told, is self-expression, individualism and our subjective "feelings." Ours is a narcissistic culture.

2. We think too highly of techniques. Because of the awesome technological achievements of our society, we tend to think that if only we can devise the right techniqes of Christian living

we will achieve what God desires of us. We even search for "Christian" formulas of success and happiness. But this never really works. The Way of Life is to "put on Christ" in deepest humility. This is the way of wisdom, and there are no hands-on exercises for learning it. Only Christ can teach us. Wisdom was in fact in the early Church, and before, a name for Christ. Throughout the book of Proverbs "wisdom" means Christ, who is prefigured in all of the Old Testament. Hagia Sophia, the name of the great Church in Byzantine Constantinople, means "Holy Wisdom." Christianity is not just "religion," which can mean merely a pious belief to which we give intellectual and emotional assent, but a comprehensive and exacting *commitment* of our lives to Holy Wisdom – Christ.

3. In our culture, "high-mindedness" is generally more esteemed than the humility of obedience to Christ. In fact, the Christian faith is sometimes thought of as nothing more than a help to "high-mindedness." This is traceable to philosophical "idealism," especially that of Plato, which we will discuss later. Our culture has been more influenced by pagan philosophy than by Christianity. Moreover, philosophy has repeatedly invaded the Christian faith, distorting it and diluting its authority. Our tendency is to take the plain words of scripture and translate them into philosophical modes of thinking that we can accept or reject, because they pose no life-or-death issues for us. We tend to regard a sentence such as the opening one of *The Didache* as a kind of hyperbolic metaphor – fine poetic words that don't really mean what they say. Over and over we treat the words of scripture the same way. Unthinkingly, we discount them: "Great ideas! I agree with them!" This enables us to evade the truth, because we don't want to take the voltage of the real thing. High-mindedness is a pseudo-Christian idealism. It ultimately fails. In Chapter Eleven we will review further some of the mischief wrought by philosophy among Christian believers.

4. "High-mindedness" failing us, we become superficial, fearful of the depths of the mystery of God's action in our midst. Our worship becomes sentimental. We settle for "self-help" sermons and simpering, self-centered songs. We seek to be grati-

fied: juveniles with fun and games, grown-ups with cheap grace – easy ways to wealth and blessings, with a quick psychiatric fix thrown in, and a religious "high" for good measure, all in a "Christian" context. We want the best of the faith in a pill, and the pill in a plastic package, and some churches are glad to oblige, for it brings in money. Yet all this is a false promise and a dead end, and there is not power, no real joy, and nothing of heaven in it. It produces lukewarmness towards Christ. It generates that attitude of mind that C. S. Lewis in *The Screwtape Letters* calls "Christianity and . . . [2] – as if Christ himself needed to have "something added," or as if we must have Christ and everything else we can lay our hands on besides. But he said, "My grace is sufficient for you . . . " (2 Corinthians 12.9)[3] and " . . . seek *first* his [God's] kingdom and his righteousness, and all these things shall be yours as well" (Matthew 6.33). Always, our society is trying to persuade us that the veneer is the real thing. We are possessed of a colossal capacity to miss the point, or to evade it. We must keep ourselves alert to this.

We will not dwell very much on these obstacles. We need only be aware of them as we study the way of love and obedience to him that Christ wants us to take.

The Way of LIfe

The way we are seeking is *life in Christ*, obedient to him, conjoined and identified with his life. It is a life that is hard-muscled, masculine and strong. It is equally tender and sensitive, perceptive and feminine. The two, however, are not blurred but distinct, each manifesting its own inherent beauty and power. There is no secret about it. The Way of Life is open to all.

Many devout Christians throughout history have shown the way. However, the early teachers of the Church are of special importance, because they were closest to our Lord in time and thought and understanding, and they knew what they were talking about, for they risked their very lives for him. Yet they are so little quoted today that their insights seem almost new. We will refer to them for the sake of their authority, depth and freshness. These teachers of the Church saw three requisites for following the Way of Life:

1. *Love* for God, for ourselves, for one another, and for his Church.

2. Conscious and continuous *obedience* to the commands of Jesus. (There are about 150 of these, but we will not be able to cover them all.)

3. *Life in his Church*, for it is only in the company of our fellow Christians, mutually supported by prayer, that the Way of Life is to be found. There is no such thing as a Church-less Christian.

We will discover that all three of these are interconnected, each implying the other two. Out of obedience we learn love, and love grows. Out of love we learn more of obedience, and obedience grows. With our fellow Christians we form one body, the Church, and in this body we learn and practice obedience, and worship God, showing our love for him and for one another, as Jesus commanded. Thus obedience and love define the Way of Life.

* * * * *

Before going further we must enter a note of caution. We have said that we will bring to bear in our study insights from the early teachers of the Church and from Eastern Orthodoxy. In the minds of many in the West, these are identified with a certain "spirituality" or "mysticism." "Eastern Christian spirituality," in fact, threatens to become almost another cult in the West. We are beginning to romanticize the lives of the "Desert Fathers," which were anything *but* romantic. They consisted of self-denial, a very costly kind of love, and the hard and thankless (it must have seemed) work of continual prayer.

I could wish even that the words *spiritual* and *mystical* might be abolished, or at least a long moratorium declared on their use, for in our usage they have bcome obstacles to understanding the Way of Life, the way of love and obedience. "Spiritual" carries the connotations of bodiless, metaphysical, nonmaterial, other-worldly, and so on. It is possible to become so "spiritual" that one does not even notice one's suffering, bleeding neighbor. But Eastern Christianity is precisely not that; it is nuts-and-bolts faith. When we pray, "Our Father who art in heaven . . . " are we being "spiritual"? Are we being "mystical"? Or are we being simply practical, realistic, and *obedient* to our Lord? Love in obedience, and obedience in love are not illuminated for us by calling them "mystical" or "spiritual"; they are simply the practice of Godly realism. Arbitrary categories are over and over again a handicap to Christian understanding, as we will see, especially in Chapter Eleven. I say this mainly to emphasize that experiences that may (with caution) properly be called "spiritual" or "mystical" are not something to be sought after for purposes of our own satisfaction but are accorded us as the result of long practice in obedience and self-giving love.

There is nothing "escapist" about Eastern Christianity. What it has to contribute is the dimension of depth and singleminded seriousness so frequently lacking in the West. If we wish to observe it in practice, one of the best places today would be the prison camps of the Soviet Union, where the Holy Eucharist may be celebrated secretly by an incarcerated priest and several fellow prisoners behind the facade of a card game — hardly a "spiritual" setting; where inmates must daily and hourly in love forgive their tormentors; where those condemned for their faith are daily dying as new martyrs; and where all minister to one another, regardless of denominational background. The sacraments and liturgies of the East are simply the formulas, derived from Christ's commands, for our human realization of him in our midst as life and resurrection in a world of sorrow and death.

There is a huge amount for us to learn from the desert fathers about the Way of Life, but let us not fantasize about them. Joy they had, but not "the good life" as we tend to think of it. *Our* desert is the world of computers, space shuttles and fast cars; of drugs, alcohol and flamboyant sex; of autonomous, depersonalized selves acting out lives of flagrant disobedience to God. This is the context in which we today are to heed the commands to love and obey and perform the *work* of liturgy and prayer, following the Way of Life. Let us study this now in the light of the commands of Jesus.

Notes

[1]We have avoided the word *myth* because for so many it carries the unfortunate implication of "not true." A "myth" is the racial memory of a pre-historic experienced reality. Its importance lies less in its cursory account of events than in the depths of meaning they contain.

[2] C. S. Lewis, *The Screwtape Letters* (New York, 1956), p. 126.

[3]Scripture passages are from *The Revised Standard Version* (New York, 1953), except as noted.

A.
TO LOVE IS
TO OBEY GOD

Chapter Two
THE NATURE OF LOVE

The nature of love is to be obedient.

This is startling doctrine to modern ears. Everything around us – television, our schools, advertising, our entire secular culture – is telling us that we do not have to be obedient to anything but ourselves. It is telling us that achievement, fulfillment, the attainment of all our desires and ambitions is to be found through our self-assertion.

Yet all of us in our deepest selves desire to love, to receive the love of others, and to know a way of life that is fruitful, rewarding and joyous. If we are not to find that fulfillment in self-assertion, then how? The answer is that we find it in the humility of obedience.

C. S. Lewis in the third volume of his space trilogy shows us an attractive young couple named Jane and Mark Studdock. Mark, an ambitious scholar, falls in with a group of "scientific humanists" out to remake the world after their own model. Jane, a "modern" woman, has ambitions of her own. The ardor of the marriage relationship fades. A tragedy develops as the humanist cabal marches to its inevitable end. Jane takes refuge among a saintly group headed by Mr. Fisher-King, a Christ figure. To him she confesses that she cannot seem to submit herself to the needs of her husband, and she attributes this to lack of love. Mr. Fisher-King tells her, "...you do not fail in obedience through lack of love, but have lost love because you never attempted obedience."[1] We will return to the Studdocks several times later on.

The connection between obedience and love is a profound theological insight. Unless one is obedient to the proper authority of another and unless one is committed to serve the real needs and requirements (not whims or manipulations) of the other, one does not love that person.

Unfortunately, our sinful, fallen nature is such that we cannot just decide we are going to commit ourselves to love, and do it. Some of us may be so fortunate in our parents that we have already experienced love and so have an innate sense of what it is all about; or we may have seen it in others whom we admire, and they provide a model for us to copy. That helps. Most of us, however, are so bogged down in our sinful willfulness that we need help no human can give. We receive that help from God through obedience to him.

We Begin with Obedience to God

The Jews, by the time of the coming of Jesus, had long been trained by God in obedience to him, though many had fallen away from obedience. Jesus, the Son of God, came reasserting the commands of God to his people and proclaiming new commands to govern not only the Jews but the ordering of all human affairs. Some of the Jews (who had grown very self-assertive) baited him, asking, "Teacher, which is the great commandment in the law" (Matthew 22.36)? In other words, "What is the fundamental basis of human affairs? On what rests the Way of Life?"

Jesus, quoting Deuteronomy 6.5, answered, "You shall love the Lord your God with all your heart, and with all your soul, and with all your mind" (Matthew 22.37). In short, total commitment to God, in love. This is the foremost of Jesus' commands.

Earlier, Jesus had been taken by Satan and tempted: "And the devil took him up, and showed him all the kingdoms of the world in a moment of time, and said to him, 'To you I will give all this authority and their glory; . . . If you . . . will worship me, it shall all be yours' " (Luke 4.5-7). "And Jesus answered him, 'It is written, you shall worship the Lord your God, and him only shall you serve [obey]' " (Luke 4.8). Again Jesus was quoting from Deuteronomy, reasserting God's command long since laid down to the Jewish people.

To begin to appreciate fully the connection between loving God and obeying him, we need to consider the word *worship*. This is a word that has had its original meaning distorted. To most of us it means a religious ceremony. Many moderns, of course, think that they are so emancipated as to worship nothing. But consider the root meaning of *worship*, which is, simply, "to accord worth" – i.e. *worth-ship*. It means to decide what has priority, what has the highest value to us. It is as unavoidable as making up our minds what clothes to put on or what to have for breakfast; we must decide *for* something and *against* something else. What do we choose? Stars of TV and sports? Food? Dress? Cars? Beautiful homes? Or perhaps we regard these things simply because they enhance *us*, and ours being a narcissistic culture, it is *ourselves* that we worship. In any event Jesus says that none of this will do. We are to accord the *highest* worth to God the Father who made us. We do that by loving and obeying him in every aspect of our lives.

We need now to consider precisely what we are talking about when we speak of "love."

Love is another word that has become distorted through careless usage. We use it today for everything from the most sublime of relationships to the most casual indulgence of physical passions. Small wonder that the nature of love is little understood in our modern world.

We need to distinguish at least two kinds of love for which the Greeks had separate words: *agape* (ah'-ga-pay) and *eros*. *Agape* is the selfless love that concerns itself more with another's good than with its own. *Eros* stresses yearning, longing, desire. It implies today romantic love, passionate desire culminating in sexual fulfillment. It often has (though it should not) a great deal of self in it and eager concern for its own personal satisfaction.

Agape

The word Jesus used over and over is *agape*. This is the kind of love that desires and seeks, and welcomes back that which was lost (as in the story of the Prodigal Son in Luke 15). It is the love that makes a unity out of many (1 Corinthians 12.12).

It is not an emotion. Emotion may accompany it, but it is not the essential element. This is reasonable if we will but think about it. For to our fallen natures this kind of love does not come spontaneously, and how can we create emotions or stir up feelings we do not have? It is impossible.

Rather, *agape* implies a decision, a commitment, an act of will, of *obedience* to God by which we renounce and put behind us all concern for our petty selves (petty indeed, in the light of the majesty of God's creation), and decide to care devoutly for God and for others for whom he has commanded us to be concerned. (Love for our neighbor we will discuss in Chapter 9).

In calling us to this kind of love God honors our dignity as free individuals. It would not be so if he simply left our attitude toward him and others prey to our involuntary sentiments and passions. Feelings and emotions may follow, but they are not the starting point. The early teachers of the Church were in fact unanimous in saying that we must renounce passions, that *agape* is without passion, that "passion is an impulse of the soul contrary to nature," for it is disobedient to God, and our proper nature is to be obedient. This is in sharp contrast to secular psychology and philosophy, including the pagan Greek philosophy of Jesus' time. The contrast will be increasingly apparent as we go along.

For as we open ourselves to God's love and receive it, and grow in our love for him, our reward is not passion but *joy*, which is a rich sense of peace and spiritual well-being. Joy is also a far thing from "getting high on Jesus," which is simply a human emotional jag.

How then do we recognize *agape*? We recognize it not by verbal definition but by what it does. We see it in tenderness, in a person's profound concern for others, especially those nearest him. We perceive it in mercy, a desire to heal and reconcile, in a desire to give, and in willingness to hope in the face of apparent hopelessness. It is manifest in our trust in Jesus Christ and in his Father and in the Holy Spirit – a trust that outweighs every fear, to the extent of surrendering life itself, at whatever cost in pain, for the sake of the good.

Agape is more considerate of the feelings of others than of its own. It is utterly forgetful of self. It is more elated over others' accomplishments than its own. It is patient, kind, thoughtful, generous, understanding, gracious, and forgiving. It endures and perseveres. *Agape* offers to do what is required. It is sensitive to *real* needs. It desires the truth. It is open, thoughtful, mature and intelligent. In its simplicity it is child*like* but never child*ish*.

Agape does not demand comfort as a right. It gives up cherished indulgences and turns its back on frivolous enjoyments. *Agape* comes from God. He initiates it. The love we express is but a reflection of the love with which he loves us. He gives it freely to all who will accept it in humility. It is a gift, for on earth we have nothing of our own from which to generate it, but only a capacity to accept it from God and render it back to him. We are told, "We love, because he first loved us" (1 John 4.19). And, "In this is love, not that we loved God but that he loved us . . . " (1 John 4.10). As one of the greatest of the early teachers put it, " . . . God accomplishes in us, as his instruments, every action and contemplation, virtue and knowledge, victory and wisdom, goodness and truth, so that we bring absolutely nothing into it from ourselves except a disposition of desiring the good."[2]

Thus our recognition of love and our impulse toward it have their source in God. Fallen as we are, we rediscover love when we turn our wills to God and let him make us channels of *his* love. Yet even in this we are not left on our own. God has sent us an example, his supreme gift to us: Jesus Christ, his son. The very love we have described is the love we find in Jesus Christ, who, having a will of his own, voluntarily surrendered it to his Father in humble obedience (John 4.34), just as we are commanded to do. We are to identify ourselves with him. This goes beyond imitation. As St. Paul says, "For as many of you as were baptized into Christ have *put on* Christ" (Galatians 3.27). All love is in Christ, for he was God become man, in human flesh yet in perfect unity with God, and God is love. (1 John 4.8). He said, "I and the Father are one" (John 10.30).

And, "He who has seen me has seen the Father . . . " (John 14.9).

This love of God for us in and through his son is a living process now, not just something that happened in history. It goes on and on, and "now" is but the beginning that stretches into eternity. Or, rather, it is the mystery of eternity entering into time at this very moment. This is not speculation but *fact*, a fact defying philosophical analysis, but established by the perceptions and testimony of unimpeachable witnesses.

Jesus said, "If you love me you will obey my commands" (John 14.15 – not RSV, but a faithful rendering of the Greek). We see now how thoroughly obedience and love are linked. A corollary, in fact, to this command would be, "If you keep my commands you will love me." There is no "logical" proof for this. Only experience can show it. But the testimony of scripture and of the Church through the centuries bears it out.

The commands of Jesus that we have noted thus far – loving God, serving, worshipping, obeying him – show us the beginning of the Way of Life. In the light of these we will appreciate more fully the other commands we are to study, and as we study those we will appreciate these more fully. First, however, let us consider *eros*.

Eros

Eros, as we have noted, stresses sexual desire, the fulfillment of romantic passion. This is the kind of love most of us in the West are trained to. The seductive smile, the well-shaped figure, the ardent embrace confront us at every turn, play on our sensibilities, stir up passions, and tell us "This is *it!*" Legends and stories such as that of Tristan and Isolde and of Romeo and Juliet clutch at our hearts as they show us the ways of erotic love, which culminate, usually, in an indulgence of the senses – and tragic death. Because of all that, the puritan Christian tradition of the West has condemned erotic love.

But can a thing that is so deeply a part of our human make-up and so beautiful to us in its expression be bad? Not in the view of the early teachers of the Church. *Eros* as the expression of ardent longing they perceived as coming from God. Some even spoke of the divine as an "erotic force," because God ardently yearns for us, and we for him. One of them states that God produces an inward state of intense longing in those receptive to him, for he "thirsts to be thirsted for, longs to be longed for, and loves to be loved."[3] Since we are made in the image of God is it surprising, then, that we should yearn after one of our own kind? Are we to attribute to evil those impulses which lead to the procreation of humankind, so gloriously made in the image of God?

For us moderns this requires some explanation. Is this teacher saying that *eros*, that ardent desire boy feels for girl, and she for him, is *of God*? Emphatically *yes*! Does this mean that we are therefore to follow wherever the impulse may lead? No. It is precisely because *eros* is so glorious a gift from God that he means us to treasure, not squander it, and to render it back to him in loving obedience. *It belongs to him.* So valuable a gift is it that he instructs us in exactly how he wants us to use it. He therefore ordained marriage, that *eros* might be fulfilled in a lifetime commitment to another person. For a monk or a nun *eros* may energize a life or service in which *eros* merges into *agape* in passionate concern for others. Its exercise in obedience to him God rewards with unspeakable joy. Its exercise in *dis*obedience generates a depressing guilt, a consequence that should hardly surprise us since it violates God's ordained Way of Life. Lust is ruled out, for it is the perversion of *eros* to our own self-gratification in disobedience to God. Its end is not love but hatred for God and our fellow men (and women) – and death. The word *eros* unfortunately does not appear in the New Testament,[4] though it implies aspiration toward that which is good and desirable, for already pagan Greek thought had appropriated it as a word for licentious passion, so the New Testament writers refused to use it. Its value as a Christian concept, however, remains.

Agape is by definition obedient love, and it is powerful for it contains the power of God. *Eros* also is powerful, but it *can* be exercised in *dis*obedience, and in disobedience it is a way of death. Obedient love is a theophany – Christ in our midst. Persons who are *in love* are of truth *in God*, and God in them.

   Do we begin to perceive now the radical meaning of love and obedience? Radical in the sense that they are to govern absolutely every facet of our life and thought? This is required, if we are to establish in ourselves the Way of Life. As St. Paul put it, " . . . bringing into captivity every thought to the obedience of Christ" (2 Corinthians 10.5).[5] And in Hebrews 2.8, " . . . putting everything in subjection under his [Christ's] feet." Let us not think that these are just pious thoughts. They mean what they say: *everything*, if truly we desire the way of love. But the devil is subtle. He plays on our egos. He tries to destroy our humility before God, saying in effect, "Well, Old Boy, so you've put yourself in the hands of God, professing love and obedience. Isn't that just great! Not let's see if *he* really loves *you*. Try him out!" In order to appreciate fully what it means to love and obey God completely we have to be aware of how we tempt God. For even Jesus did not escape but was cajoled by the devil to try to tempt his Father.

Tempting God

   In the fourth chapter of Matthew we have the account of the devil's taking Jesus up to a high point of the Temple and telling him to throw himself down, since God had promised (in Psalm 91) that angels would support him, "lest you dash your foot against a stone." And Jesus answered him, "You shall not tempt the Lord your God" (Matthew 4.7). (We had better not think, incidentally, that just because this was addressed to the devil it was not meant for us.) Some modern translations instead of using "tempt" render the passage, "you shall not put your God to the test." This means that to stumble, and trust God to save us, is one thing. But deliberately to hurl ourselves into danger or to go off doing this and that on our own, trusting God to pull our chestnuts out of the fire is to seek our own destruction. God will not play our games.

   Yet we tempt God all the time in our personal behavior and with our self-righteous actions, assuming God will save us from our folly. The early teachers of the Church would be aghast at today's do-good schemes. "Are they," they would ask, "arrived at following much prayer, silence, and fasting to discern the will of the Holy Spirit?" We would have to admit that for the most part they are not, that they are mostly concocted in political caucuses and "centers of learning" not notable for prayer, silence and fasting. Again and again we tempt God, saying to him in effect, "Look at all the good things I am doing! Back me up!" But well-meant schemes do not serve God unless they are done in obedience and love.

There are those who will immediately object, "But you are saying that we are bound by a law of obedience. Jesus came to set us free from the law he laid down for the Jews in the Old Testament, so that we can *act* and *progress*! True, we are free, but there is a worse bondage than submission to any "law," and that is slavery to our self-conceit. The Great Lie practiced everywhere today is: *Man is God.* But the truth is that *God* is God, and we "do the truth" (John 3.21; 1 John 4.16) only by loving and *obeying* him. God is no killjoy; obedience to Jesus' commands is pure delight, for he said, "These things I have spoken to you, that my joy may be in you, and that your joy may be full" (John 15.11). This is a paradox of the Christian faith: only in obedience can we have the joy of perfect freedom (John 8.36).

Seeking Perfection

Finally, we must consider a command of Jesus that has to do directly with the nature of love. It is the nature of love to seek perfection – wholeness, completion, fulfillment. Jesus said, "You, therefore, must be perfect, as your heavenly Father is perfect" (Matthew 5.48).

Of all Jesus' commands this is the one we are perhaps most likely to treat as no more than a pious exhortation. "Counsels of perfection" we use as an epigram for impossible advice. How can we be perfect? But we treat this too lightly. Perfection is the end result of love and obedience to God.

It is that and more. The earliest Christian teachers perceived

Jesus' command as directing us to enter into a process of *deifi-cation* (Greek, *theosis*). To our ears this is shocking, if not blasphemous. "*Me* deified?" we ask in disbelief. But God means business. We are indeed to become *like him*. For man was created by God in his own image, and in spite of our having fallen away he insists that the image must be restored to its original perfection. *We are meant to be living icons of God!* As the Apostle Peter said, we are to "become partakers of the divine nature" (2 Peter 1.4).

Yet of ourselves we cannot accomplish that restoration. It is accomplished only by Jesus Christ, who by *his deity* united with *his humanity* can *deify us*. As St. Paul said, we *put on* Christ, we become identified with him through obedience and love. One of the greatest of the early teachers of the Church, Irenaios (A.D. 133-200), puts it in an aphorism that has echoed down the ages throughout Christendom: "God became man that man might become God." It is not an easy process, nor is it perfectly accomplished in this life. However, he left us a sacrament in which we are united with him. He commanded us to *eat his flesh* and to *drink his blood*, and he said, "He who eats my flesh and drinks my blood abides in me, and I in him" (John 6.56). This is the sacrament of the Eucharist, or Holy Communion, which we will discuss in Chapter 10. In this is the mystery of conversion, of "deification," and it occurs in love, and *only in love*. Jesus wished to save the Pharisees and the Sadducees and the whole of the Jewish people, but their hearts were dull and hard (Matthew 13.15); they would not have love, and without love they could not be "born again."

We have begun to understand now something of the nature of love. We will understand more as we go along.

Let us return to Jane Studdock, whom we mentioned at the beginning of this chapter. Her husband, Mark, escaped from the debacle of the humanist experiment and went to St. Anne's, where Jane's Christian group was located – and promptly undressed and went to bed in the guesthouse that had been prepared. Jane went to be with him. The story does not imply that thenceforth she was obedient to every whim and fancy of his.

Rather, her spirit was changed. Jane, already repentant, desired now to put selfish ambition behind her and to live with Mark in love and obedience to the requirements of the marriage relationship ordained by God. And the story ends with Venus (*eros*) reigning over the night and radiating the glory of God.

Notes

[1]C. S. Lewis, *That Hideous Strength* (New York, 1946), p. 147.

[2]Maximos the Confessor (A.D. 580-662) in E. Kadloubovsky and G. E. H. Palmer, trans., *Early Fathers from the Philokalia* (London, 1954), p. 376.

[3]Maximos the Confessor in G. E. H. Palmer, Philip Sherrard and Kallistos Ware, trans. and eds., *The Philokalia, the Complete Text*, Vol. 2 (London, 1979), p. 67. *Philokalia* means "love of the beautiful." It implies, however, something transcendent, exalted, excellent, leading to our illumination, purification and perfection. The books cited here are collections of Greek texts written between the fourth and fifteenth centuries. They first appeared in English in 1953 in two volumes: *Early Fathers from the Philokalia* and *Writings from the Philokalia on the Prayer of the Heart*. The British publisher is now issuing a new translation in five volumes of the entire original Greek text.

[4]Another word for "love" – one that appears eighteen times in the New Testament, – is *philia*, which stresses the aspect of warm friendship or personal affection. It occurs, for example, in John 21.15-17 when Jesus asks Peter if he loves him – using *agape*. Peter answers using *philia*. For our purposes the difference is not one that need concern us. Our focus is on *agape*.

[5]*King James (Authorized) Version*, hereinafter designated in the text *KJV*.

Chapter Three

TO LOVE JESUS IS TO FOLLOW HIM

As we enter into the mystery of love, we become increasingly aware of how much love desires to be united with the beloved – in its company, conversing with it, sharing with it, following it. It is hardly surprising, therefore, to find that he who loves us more even than we love ourselves commands us, *"Follow me."* Jesus repeats this command more often than any other, and since his commands were not just to those around him two thousand years ago but *for all time*, the directive to *follow him* has an equally compelling urgency for us today. The various commands to "follow," to "come," or to be in union with him occur nearly a dozen times in the gospels (not counting duplications), and we should not be surprised that it is John, "the beloved disciple," who gives them special emphasis. The gospel of John, in fact, significantly begins (Chapter 1) and ends (Chapter 21) with commands by Jesus to *follow*.

A Life of Action

The life of a Christian is to be a life of action – obedience in love. Never does Jesus say, "Sit down and correlate what I am saying with your own philosophical understanding." He never uttered a philosophical speculation (though many theologians and churchmen coming after him have), nor any encouragement to others to speculate. He simply, as one with authority (Mark 1.22), told his followers what to do. This may be the reason why the *gospel*, which means the "good news" of God's fulfillment of his prophecy of a savior in the person of his own flesh and blood son, is "hidden from the wise and clever" (those of a philo-

-35-

sophical, speculative turn of mind who think men can figure out all the answers) and is revealed to mere children (Matthew 11.25 and Luke 10.21). This does not mean that we are not to ponder what Jesus said. On the contrary, we are to think about it all the time. It means, rather, that we are to put aside our intrusive, speculative thoughts so that we may hear his commands. It is by living those commands, not speculating about them, that we learn the meaning of scripture, and in obedience to them learn to love.

When two disciples of John the Baptist (the forerunner, who came to "prepare the way" for Christ) heard John say, "Behold the lamb of God," meaning Jesus, who was to be God's sacrifice for man, they immediately went after Jesus and asked him where he was staying, and he told them, "Come and see" (John 1.39). The next day Jesus went into Galilee and found Philip and again said, simply, "Follow me" (John 1.43).

Similarily, after the resurrection, Jesus foretells Peter's own crucifixion, then commands him, "Follow me" (John 21.19). Did he mean into death by crucifixion and on to his resurrection? Yes, and into heaven, as we shall see. Only two verses later, Peter, walking with Jesus and possessed of our human bent for speculation and curiosity about the future, asks Jesus what is going to happen to the "beloved disciple," and Jesus sharply answers, " . . . what is that to you? Follow me!"

So it is with us. These commands are for us, not only for Jesus' immediate disciples, for we also are disciples. We are to "come and see" (or "taste and see," as Psalm 34.8 tells us). We are to act. We are to follow Jesus. What God's plans are for others is none of our business. We are to obey orders, *then* we will discover what discipleship is all about, and love.

The earliest teachers in the Church took this with utmost seriousness, and "obedience" is the keynote of their entire thought. They did not speculate, theorize or philosophize. This in fact is one of the major points of departure from the early Church by Western thinkers who, heavily influenced by pagan Greek thought, gave themselves over to a huge amount of speculation and philosophical elaboration in theological matters, to the grief of the Church and Christians everywhere, as we shall see in Chapter 11.

But the would-be Christian often thinks, "I'm too old; after my long, black record I can never catch up. I cannot follow." Nonsense! Scripture assures us that it is never too late: Abraham was 75 years old when he set forth from Ur in obedience to God (Genesis 12.4), and those who begin to follow (work) at the eleventh hour (meaning us) get the same reward as the Apostles themselves, who were first (Matthew 20.9). Also, we are not to look longingly back at our old life and be reduced to a heap of lifeless rock as was Lot's wife (Genesis 19.26), but having started on our course we are to stick with it, or we will not be fit for the kingdom of heaven that is promised us when we follow Christ (Luke 9.62). Tito Colliander, a superb modern teacher in the Orthodox tradition, puts it vividly, "You have cast off your old humanity; let the rags lie."[1]

In practical terms, what does this mean for us today? Jesus spells it out.

We Are to Follow in All Circumstances

Obedient to love's commands, and learning more of love as we obey, we are to follow Jesus even when this may seem illogical.

One of Jesus' followers received news that his father had died, and he asked leave of Jesus to go and bury his father. Jesus answered him, "Follow me, and leave the dead to bury their own dead" (Matthew 8.22). To the disciple this must have been a terrible answer. Not to honor the dead? This from the Son of God, the very God who commanded us to honor father and mother? No, but something different. Jesus was announcing that discipleship is a whole new way of life. In following the new, we must put the old behind us. This does not mean that as a rigid rule we are not to see to the burial of parents. The meaning, however, is clear enough. There is a death and we go back for the funeral, and if the family situation is not under the discipline of a Christian commitment, it is likely to be chaotic: mental and emotional, if not actual physical, conflict; arguments over arrangements; mutual recriminations about the terminal illness; bitter controversies over inheritance; anger; tension; spiritual uproar. It happened in those days, and it happens now. This can be devastating for the new Christian, as Jesus knew; hence his prohibition. For the sake of discipleship, we had best simply walk away from certain situations that may cause us to stumble, and in which we can do no good.

On another occasion the disciples were in a boat on the Sea of Galilee, which is prone to sudden, violent storms. Jesus had gone up into the hills to pray after a strenuous night of preaching. A storm came up, and the boat was "beaten by waves; for the wind was against them" (Matthew 14.24). (Are our lives not also beaten by waves?) Some time between 3:00 and 6:00 a.m. they saw a figure walking on the water and were terrified, but Jesus identified himself, and Peter said, "Lord, if it is you, bid me come to you on the water." And Jesus commanded him, "Come" (Matthew 14.29). Note that Peter *asked* to be commanded – we are not heedlessly to hurl ourselves into danger (as we saw in the preceeding chapter) even to go to Jesus, but we wait for his command. Peter went, then began to sink, and Jesus reached out and saved him.

To those who have not made a commitment to obedience in love, this is a dubious, if interesting, story. But to anyone who has totally committed his fate to Christ in a life or death situation, even if but for a moment, the story has a stunning reality. By faith, Peter walked on the water, started to sink, and was saved. So it is with us every day in situations where by natural expectations we should expect to be lost – provided we act in faith, obedient to commands, and *ask Jesus to save us.*

The Fathers of the Church were intensely aware of this. Their very lives were to them from moment to moment a miracle. In spiritual sinkings, as well as in physical danger, they again and again cried out to God. Colliander puts it as follows: "Do not pity yourself, seek comfort in nothing but your cry to the Lord: *Haste thee, O God, to deliver me! Make haste to help me, O Lord*" (Psalm 70.1). "You cannot expect any real help from any other source."[2]

There are two other commands that we must consider carefully if we are to follow Jesus in love.

The first has to do with Jesus' cross. Jesus said, "If any man would come after me, let him deny himself and take up his cross . . . " (Matthew 16.24). Strictly, this could be merely the statement of a condition for discipleship. There are similiar passages in Luke 14.27 and 17.33 and in John 12.25. It amounts, however, to a command. Jesus is saying: *this is what you must do if you love me and want to follow me.*

Do what? Starve, reject, kill off, *crucify* your old, natural pagan self, with all its cravings, personal plans, appetites and ambitions, and identify yourself with Christ, putting yourself at his disposal. Many Christians misunderstand this. They speak of some irritation, hardship or inconvenience as "my cross." But that is not at all what Jesus meant. The cross is our *self*-denial; it permanently defines our relationship to the world as Christ's followers. As Saint Paul put it, " . . . the cross of our Lord Jesus Christ, by which the world has been crucified to me, and I to the world" (Galatians 6.14). If we weep and lament, that is our normal condition as Christians in the world (John 16.20). We are all in exactly the same position as Simon of Cyrene: *compelled* to bear Jesus' cross (Matthew 27.32). It is not fun, and was never meant to be. But love hangs on through death itself. God's grace does not come cheaply.

The second command is very similiar. Jesus said, "Take my yoke upon you, and learn of me . . . " (Matthew 11.29 KJV). The command is familiar to everyone, and nearly everyone gets it wrong. What we do is remember the part quoted above, then jump to v. 30, which promises, " . . . my yoke is easy, and my burden is light." Thus we reassure ourselves that the Christian life will be an easy one.

Quite the opposite. We must consider the entire passage and stress the *condition* that will make our burden light: "Take my yoke upon you and learn of me; *for I am meek and lowly in heart*; and ye shall find rest unto your souls. For my yoke is easy, and my burden is light" (KJV).

So we get to the nub of the matter, which is meekness and

a heartfelt lowliness: in a word, *humility*. After obedience to Jesus' commands, nothing received greater emphasis from the early teachers of the Church. They wrote: " . . . the root and mother of all evil is arrogance; so in the new God-man, Jesus Christ, and in those who resolve to live in his image, the origin, source, and foundation of all blessings is humility."[3]

Humility

Humility is the key to understanding and practicing obedience and love. In his parable of the marriage feast in Luke 14, Jesus says that when we are invited to the feast we are to take the lowest place. What is the "marriage feast"? Heaven – church, which we will discuss presently, and again in the last section of this book. Then we may be invited to "go up higher," for "every one who exalts himself will be humbled, and he who humbles himself will be exalted" (Luke 14.11).

Are we humble? Of course. We are Christian, are we not? So when we go to church we piously take a back seat. Of course there's Mrs. Paine up front there, who's such an annoyance to everyone, making a spectacle of herself. Thank God we're not like *her*! But this is not humility. This is pride. Humility is an interior thing. In true humility we will think *more highly of Mrs. Paine than we do of ourselves*. After all, what if God is more pleased that Mrs. Paine is in church today than that we are? Saint Paul tells us that we are in humility to count others better than ourselves (Philippians 2.3). And some of the Church's early teachers said we should count ourselves worse even than the beasts, for they follow their instincts and know no better; and worse than demons, for we are often the slaves of demons!

This is tough teaching. We desire to be first (secretly, in our hearts, if not openly). But we must examine our hearts and compel them to obey, for Jesus said, " . . . he who is least among you all is the one who is great" (Luke 9.48). This is the killing of pride. It is the crucifixion of self that we mentioned in the preceeding chapter. The technique for it is actually not too difficult: look on the other person, no matter how tedious, repulsive or difficult they are, and say inwardly – *and mean it* – "I regard him (or her) more highly than myself" (Philippians 2.3-4). You dare not risk thinking otherwise. God is the judge, and if he perceives differently, let him be the one to say, "Friend, go up higher" (Luke 14.10). In any event, you have lost nothing, for only God can lift you up; you cannot lift yourself. It is the humble heart that God most loves, as David says in Psalm 51. This is contrary to much of modern "psychology."

I am aware that there are those who suffer from what clinicians diagnose as a pathological lack of self-esteem. That is not at all the same as humility. Rather, it is a denial of the worth of the person God made, often stemming from an induced sense of guilt. Humility does not deny that worth, nor does it derive from a sense of guilt. It simply denies the *self* that would assert superiority over others or equality with God. It avoids the extremes of both pride and despair, for both dishonor God. All sense of past injury, all our sense of unworthiness, all our guilt we release to Christ in obedience and love. To wallow in despondency is to indulge our pride.

Nor is humility something that is particularly evident. A "humility" that is obvious to everyone is probably not humility at all but pride, a posture, for true humility can never be a posture or an act. But true humility does not come easily. When we find that by our own will we cannot achieve it, we must pray, "God, kill my pride, and give me the humility your son, Jesus Christ, commanded me to have." We will receive it, though at the cost of our crucifixion. But this is very satisfactory, for, as the early teachers taught, humility eradicates greed, envy, possessiveness, inordinate desire – indeed, all the major temptations of Satan. Humble, we are invulnerable, for how can we be knocked down when we never considered ourselves anything but lowly? There is tremendous spiritual relief in this, for we stop striving to win points with our fellows, and we find instead the "rest for our soul" that Jesus promised (Matthew 11.29).

Jesus himself had great humility, as we saw in his coming as King – on a donkey (Chapter 1). It was of a piece with his love and his obedience to his father. Before leaving the subject, let us consider an instance of Jesus' humility that is connected with his command to "follow."

Jesus one day came upon Matthew (the man who wrote the first gospel), a tax collector, hated by the Jews because the tax collectors were in the service of Rome and typically robbed the people. Jesus commanded him, "Follow me," and Matthew obeyed, and they went to his house, along with a lot of others whom the self-righteous Pharisee party regarded as contemptible sinners. The Pharisees asked Jesus' disciples why he consorted with such riffraff. But Jesus, hearing them, ripped off their mask of self-righteousness and commanded them (quoting Hosea 6.6), "Go and learn what this means, 'I desire mercy and not sacrifice' " (Matthew 9.13). Love, humility and mercy go together. The Pharisees relied on animal sacrifices, an outward thing, to put themselves right with God. They did not love. Jesus was proclaiming a new order that required not outward obedience but inner compliance with the *spirit* of the law, which is love, humility and mercy. If we are self-confident of our own righteousness, then we also are Pharisees, and we have not learned humility.

We must note one final danger here: we are urged over and over to *imitate* Christ, and many people get this wrong. They assume it means to set themselves up as operators and manipulators on behalf of Christ – do-gooders, crusaders for one "cause" or another. But this is to act in pride, not humility and obedience. To them Jesus will say, "I never knew you; depart from me you evildoers" (Matthew 7.23). It is in silence, prayer and fasting that God will show us what he wants us to do.

* * * * *

At the beginning of this chapter we noted that love desires above all to be united with the beloved. Thus Jesus commanded us to follow him. Now we find that he desires much more even than that. He desires us to be fully united with him. We are to become so identified with him that we exist as one with him. This is a profound mystery. It is set forth in great dominical discourse found only in John (the beloved disciple again),

Chapters 14 to 16. It follows directly after the account of the Last Supper, in which Jesus initiates the rite of Holy Communion (Eucharist), which we will consider in Chapter 10. In this he commanded that we should *eat his flesh* and *drink his blood*, meaning complete identification with him. Jesus then commands: "Be in me at all times . . . " (John 15.4)[4] and " . . . be ever in my love" (John 15.9). We have passed beyond the limits of human reason, but not of rationality, for *Jesus himself is the standard of rationality.* He is indeed the measure of everything. If we care about obedience and love, these commands must be deeply engraved in our consciousness. Jesus explains them in the metaphor of the vine and our engraftment onto it. With passages as difficult as these are for many to understand, it is often best to go to the simplest possible translation. In Basic English they are rendered as follows:

> Be in me at all times as I am in you. As the branch is not able to give fruit of itself, if it is not still on the vine, so you are not able to do so if you are not in me. I am the vine, you are the branches . . . be ever in my love. If you keep my laws [commands], and will be ever in my love, even as I have kept in my father's laws [commands], and am ever in his love.

We must consider now our destination if we follow Christ and become identified with him.

The Kingdom of Heaven

The entire aim of following Christ is to enter the kingdom of heaven. Now we are confronted with yet another mystery. Just where and when is this "kingdom," and of what does it consist? This is a mystery with which we are going to have to come to terms, if we are to understand and trust Jesus, love, obey and follow him. For "heaven" is mentioned nearly 250 times in the New Testament, and Jesus said, " . . . the kingdom of heaven is at hand" (Matthew 4.17).

Jesus in his own mind was obviously very clear about what he meant. His disciples were not. " . . . they thought that the kingdom of God [heaven] should immediately appear" (Luke 19.11 KJV). By this they meant that all evildoers, God's enemies, would be instantly overcome and from then on the goodness of God would reign throughout the world. Today many Christians are equally confused. Since evil still influences the world, we tend to think of heaven as "pie in the sky" that we will get after we die, if we are good. But neither is this satisfactory, for Jesus said, " . . . the kingdom of God [heaven] is within you" (Luke 17.21 KJV). That is, it is a *new state of being*, now embodied in his person in their midst. It is soon to be embodied in the Church, where we experience it in fellowship with others and in ourselves.

The disciples gradually discovered the truth of heaven in their experience of the Way of Life after Jesus' resurrection. As they "put on Christ" and became continually identified with him, loving him and obeying his commands, they came, individually and as a body, to experience the joy that is the essence of the kingdom of heaven. Saint Paul is the perfect example. From hating and persecuting Christians, he was transformed by Christ into an obedient lover. Out of the way of death he found the Way of Life, and in spite of all that befell him he was to write repeatedly of *joy*. His is to be our experience as well.

As Christians, we exist, then, in two worlds simultaneously. There is the world of the flesh and earthliness in which, as Jesus tells us, we are certain to have tribulation (John 16.33), but which we erroneously regard as the "real world." And there is the world of the spirit, of the kingdom of God, or heaven, a kingdom of love, *in which we already participate* through our identification with Christ. The Church in the East has always understood this and has dramatized and expressed it in their liturgy. This is truly the *real world*, for our temporal world is passing away but in Christ the new, with all its joy is both here and now, and yet to come in its full realization. All that is said of "heaven" in the New Testament can be encompassed in this framework of understanding.

Meanwhile we have a job to do. If we are to achieve the kingdom (and help others to do so) our work is cut out for us. We are given specific commands:

Jesus said, "Repent, for the kingdom of heaven is at hand" (Matthew 4.17). We have already cited the second clause of this verse; now we see that the condition for entering the kingdom is to "repent." What does this mean? Quite simply and literally, "to have another mind." It means to say *no* to our past and present thoughts or behavior that are not in accord with God's commands, and to embark on a new course in conformity with his will. Our old, sinful nature has been leading us *away* from the kingdom, which Jesus says is now "at hand," meaning "ready to enter, accessible." We are to enter after voluntarily renouncing our old pernicious ways, casting off worldly sophistication and becoming as little children.

Jesus explains this. He says, "Let the little children come to me, and do not hinder them; for to such belongs the kingdom of God. Truly, I say to you, whoever does not receive the kingdom of God like a child shall not enter it" (Luke 18.16,17). Jesus was preaching to his disciples, and Luke reports that people began to bring infants to him that he might touch them. The situation obviously was getting a bit disorderly and interfering with Jesus' preaching, so the disciples tried to stop them. But Jesus immediately told them to desist and used the children as an example. "Whoever humbles himself like this child," he said, "he is the greatest in the kingdom of heaven" (Matthew 18.4). In short, simplicity, humility and submission are conditions for acquiring and enjoying love and participating in the life of the kingdom.

There is yet another condition. We must hew to a narrow path. Jesus said, "Enter by the narrow gate; for the gate is wide and the way is easy, that leads to destruction, and those who enter by it are many. For the gate is narrow and the way is hard, that leads to life [the Way of Life], and those who find it are few" (Matthew 7.13,14). In short, since the way is hard, we have to *work* at it. At ease, we will never make it. In this connection, the early teachers of the Church continually preached what God commanded the Israelites immediately after giving them the Ten Commandments: "You shall be careful to do therefore as the Lord your God has commanded you; you shall not turn aside to the right or to the left" (Deuteronomy 5.32).

Jesus gave few direct commands concerning heaven. However, passages about the kingdom of heaven total 113 in just the four gospels, and the entire gospel of Matthew, which was written for the Jews, is constructed around the theme of the kingdom, which is what the Jews were longing for and expecting from their Messiah, though with the misconception that it was an earthly kingdom. In any event it is plain that the kingdom of heaven (or God) is our goal if we are obedient to Christ's commands to follow him. And there is where we will find love.

We Become Violent

Now a startling thing happens. Jesus suddenly says to his disciples, " . . . the kingdom of heaven has suffered violence, and men of violence take it by force" (Matthew 11.12). J. B. Philips renders the passage: " . . . the kingdom of heaven has been taken by storm and eager men are forcing their way into it."[5] In Basic English it reads, " . . . force has been used against the kingdom of heaven, and violent men take it."

What are we to make of this? How can this passage be reconciled with those that identify the kingdom as a place of peace, to be received with simplicity, humility and the submission of a little child? The gospel is full of paradoxes, but this seems to be one of the most difficult. However, in its resolution we discover an important clue to following the Way of Life.

What Jesus is saying is simply that if we decide to love, obey and follow him, we've got a battle on our hands. To achieve heaven is literally a life or death struggle. The early Church saw this clearly; our affluent societies today do not see it; yet the spiritual conditions for following the Way have not changed. Temptations beset us – more now than ever – and we have to say *no*, and it is a fight in which we are often wounded and must suffer. One part of us desires voluptuous passions, or ease and comfort, and the other God. We have to refuse the ease and comfort and trample down the passions: anger, bitterness, lustful desires, conceit, dreaminess, evasions. One fourteen-century Eastern monk specifically mentions sixty-nine of them, and there are more. These are real enemies against which we must do battle. The famous seventh-century monastic, John Klimakos ("John of the Ladder") says to flog them with the name of Jesus. This is virile, bloody stuff, not tea and sympathy. It is "keeping the body under," as Saint Paul advised. It is a battle of the mind, a matter of will and determination. And what if the battle overwhelms us? Prayer brings instant help, as we will see in the next chapter, not to remove the temptation but to enable our wills in the matter to be decisive.

Christians all around us are engaged in this battle. Are we part of it? If we do not find ourselves to be part of it, then probably we are practicing its opposite, which is *sloth.*

Sloth is little mentioned today, even in sermons, probably because it is so much a part of the spiritual landscape that we scarcely notice it. Yet sloth was regarded by the earliest Christian teachers as perhaps the greatest obstacle to those who would follow the Way of Life, for it is the opposite of the positive action we must take to follow Christ. An eminent contemporary Orthodox teacher, Alexander Schmemann, defines it as follows: "It is that strange laziness and passivity of our entire being which . . . constantly convinces us that no change is possible and therefore desirable. It is in fact a deeply rooted cynicism which to every spiritual challenge responds, 'what for?' and makes our life one tremendous spiritual waste. It is the root of all sin because it poisons the spiritual energy at its very source."[6]

There is a prayer by one of the great saints of the sixth century, Ephraim of Syria, that is used throughout the Orthodox Church during the Lenten season before Pascha (Easter). It might well be used by us all:

O Lord and Master of my life!
Take from me the spirit of sloth,

faint-heartedness, lust of power and idle talk.
But give rather the spirit of chastity, humility,
patience, and love to Thy servant.
Yea, O Lord and King!
Grant me to see my own errors and
not to judge my brother;
For Thou art blessed unto ages of ages. Amen.[7]

We must think of our own effort (if any) to follow Christ. Is there really any serious internal warfare? Is there a struggle to enter by the narrow gate? Or do we indulge our desires, cultivate self-pity, and habitually go all limp and passive and say, "I'll just be a nice guy (or gal)."

But to be just a "decent fellow" is impossible. As C. S. Lewis aptly put it, "We are like eggs at present. And you cannot go on indefinitely being just an ordinary, decent egg. We must be hatched or go bad."[8] And in the hatching process struggle is necessary, as anyone who has ever watched a chick hatching knows. Yet of ourselves it is hopeless. We need help. Most of us have a life ahead of us, and there is work to be done. If we ask Christ to help us, our victory is certain, for he has already achieved it. Christ himself tells us how to proceed – in prayer and fasting, as we will see in the next chapter. Thus the paradox of violence is resolved: we fight the "good fight," as Saint Paul says (2 Timothy 4.7) (it is, incidentally, the *only* fight there is), praying all the time in obedience and love, in patience, peace, faith and humility for the victory Christ promises.

Notes

[1] Tito Colliander, *The Way of the Ascetics* (New York, 1982), p. 3. Colliander is a contemporary Orthodox layman who has studied deeply in the early Church writers. Of Finnish descent, he was a frequent pilgrim to the great Russian monastery of Valaamo after it was forced out of Russia after the Bolshevik revolution and a remnant of monks reestablished it in Finland. This brief work is among the modern devotional classics.

[2] *Ibid.*, p. 85.

[3] E. Kadloubovsky & G. E. H. Palmer, trans., *Writings from the Philokalia on the Prayer of the Heart* (London, 1951), p. 178.

[4] *The New Testament in Basic English* (New York, 1941), hereinafter designated B in the text.

[5] J. B. Phillips, *The New Testament in Modern English* (New York, 1960), hereinafter designated P in the text.

[6] Alexander Schmemann, *Great Lent* (Crestwood, N.Y., 1969), p. 34.

[7] *Ibid.*, p. 34.

[8] C. S. Lewis, *Mere Christianity* (New York, 1956), p. 155.

Chapter Four

WE PROCEED BY PRAYER AND FASTING

In the preceeding chapter we stated that the life of a Christian is to be a life of action. We spoke of the violent struggle required to enter the new life of the kingdom of God. We noted that there is *work to be done*. What is the nature of this "work"?

In the history of the Church an argument has frequently erupted concerning "faith" *vs.* "works." Saint Paul wrote, "For by grace you have been saved through faith; and . . . not because of works . . . " (Ephesians 2.8,9). Martin Luther took this up and made it the foundation of his movement protesting the legalism of Rome. Paul was of course protesting the legalism of the Pharisees, who assumed that by "works" of obedience to Mosaic law they attained righteousness. Then James, "the brother of the Lord," writes, " . . . faith by itself, if it has no works, is dead" (James 2.17).

Many Christians today use the exhortations of James as their justification for an enormous range of government social action programs, the ultimate consequences of which they cannot possibly foresee. As usual, the early teachers of the Church took a common sense approach. Of course the Christian was, in the obedience of love for God and for his neighbor, to "feed the hungry" and "clothe the naked," as we shall see in Chapter 9. But this was to be a *personal* thing, a *self*-giving in Christ, not a vast, impersonal program, for it is clearly implied that in giving we are to give also Christ (Matthew 10.42; 25.40; Mark 9.41). But, we say to ourselves, the needs are vastly greater than any individual or even thousands of individuals can deal with. So they are. What, then, is the answer?

God's Enterprise

The answer is prayer, which is the greatest of all *works*. (Another "work," which we will consider in Chapter 10, is *liturgy*, a word derived from the same Greek roots that give us "layman" and "work.")

There is too much in life in all its various aspects and relationships for us to cope with in any earthly way. We must, of course, cope to the extent of our abilities, but even when we do, there will be much that goes awry. But Jesus said, "I will not leave you desolate; I will come to you" (John 14.18).

How does he come? He meets us in prayer. This is a real point of identification with him, for he himself prayed continually. It is in prayer that we become "like" Jesus, one with him; it is in prayer that the process of "deification" that we spoke of in the preceeding chapter goes on. In prayer we "put on" Christ. The Christian lives by constant prayer (1 Thessalonians 5.17). In this God invites us to participate in his own enterprise, the most important in all creation. In prayer we follow Christ. In prayer we enter the kingdom of heaven. Let us beware of calling this "mystical"; "realism" *vs.* "mysticism" is a false dichotomy, for what we blandly dismiss as "mystical" is the real; it is the earth that is passing away (Matthew 24.35). Prayer for the Christian *is reality*. It becomes our *entire* life, our *only* life, our *real* life. It is, to put it colloquially, precisely "where the rubber meets the road."

That God should tolerate, invite, indeed *command* our participation in so great an enterprise is an utterly tremendous thing. Yet here we are, called to adore him, to confess to him our sins (for he takes them away), to thank him (astounding, that God should invite us to be so close to him as to enable us to express a word of thanks to him as we would to a friend who has served us a fine dinner), to intercede with him for others (intolerable compliment, that he should accord us that great a responsibility), and to petition him for our own needs. How are we to do so great a thing? Jesus left specific instructions in the form of commands which, if we love him (and we must, for *he is our own good*), we will obey. Let us consider them.

How to Pray

Jesus said, " . . . when you pray you must not be like the hypocrites . . . " (Matthew 6.5); " . . . go into you room and shut the door . . . " (Matthew 6.6) " . . . in praying do not heap up empty phrases . . . " (Matthew 6.7) " . . . whenever you stand praying, forgive . . . " (Mark 11.25); and, "Pray then like this" (Matthew 6.9).

Jesus begins by condemning the religious show-offs of his day, who "love to stand and pray in the synagogues and at the street corners, that they may be seen of men." He calls them "hypocrites," for they are not praying to glorify God but only themselves. He instructs us to pray in private (including, of course, the privacy of corporate prayer among Christians). He rules out the chatter of the pagan Gentiles, "who heap up mighty phrases," thinking "they will be heard for their many words." We are, rather, to pray simply and directly to the Father, and he gives his disciples then "the Lord's prayer."

The clauses of this prayer (Matthew 6.9-13) are so familiar that their awesome implications for us as we seek to follow the Way of Life tend to escape us. Jesus' words command the attitude we are to have toward God, toward our neighbor, and toward ourselves with respect to our particular needs.

Jesus begins with "our Father." Immediately we have to note some understandings that have been lost over the years or are even now being grossly distorted in some Church circles. Jesus addressed God as "father." This means no more, and no less, than what it says. God was his actual father, just as each one of us had or has an actual father on earth. The word is not a metaphor; it is *literal*. Mary was Jesus' mother. Today we have a "new lectionary" from the National Council of Churches, which includes God also as "mother." This would be ludicrous, were it not so tragic. It is undeniably blasphemous. This is not "interpretation" of scripture but its destruction and replacement with a concoction of nonsense.

Note Mark 14.36. Jesus said, "Abba, Father . . . "*Abba* was the common Aramaic (the ordinary language of Palestine in

Jesus' time) word that Jewish children used when they spoke
to their fathers. It means *daddy*. If this sounds scandalous to
us, it sounded far more scandalous to the Jews of Jesus' time.
Here was a man, an ordinary man (they thought), calling *God*
"daddy"! That is why they killed Jesus (Luke 22.70,71).

Why then does Jesus command us to say, "*our* Father"?
Because Jesus was proclaiming our adoption by God as sons.
All those who believe in Christ, identifying themselves with him,
are to become his siblings, literally *children* of God. We are to
be God's sons (and daughters) as if our earthly father had died
in our childhood and we were legally adopted by another man
to stand in place of our physical father. We are, with and in
Christ, to cry "*abba, daddy!*" (See Romans 8.15 and Galatians
4.6). God's actions and the words of scripture are simple, plain
and straightforward.

There are those, of course, who have so suffered at the
hands of their earthly fathers that the very thought of calling
God "father" is repugnant. But God is not limited or corrupted
by earthly mischances. He asks us to accept fully and trustfully
his substitution of himself for the earthly fathers we have experienced. It is not blasphemous, but acceptable and even desirable
when we pray "our Father" to think in our minds: *papa! daddy!*
He loves us that much, and in exactly that *personal* way.

Before we leave this, there is one other aspect we must consider. If we are ourselves earthly fathers, God by his action in
fathering Jesus Christ has made *us* icons of himself. This requires some reflection. It is an appalling thought. We are not
just sires of such and such offspring whom we can treat as we
wish. As fathers, we are in the *image of God!* God so perceives
us. And so do our children. Begetting is not just an act we can
do, then walk away from. It thrusts us into the position of being
living images of the living God! We are to love our children exactly as God the Father loves his son, Jesus. It is an awesome
responsibility, and we cannot possibly evade it. Woe then to
the father who abandons his children, or to the mother who
drives her children's father away, or to the man who assents
to the abortion of the fetus he fathered, for all these actions are

in contradiction to God's established order and commands, and the perpetrators will suffer – but forgiveness is still possible, as we shall see.

"Heaven" and "thy kingdom," which are the same thing, we have already discussed in the preceding chapter. It is a place, whether a physical location or a place of the spirit, we are not told. If it comes to pervade the entire earth, then its place is earth, though not limited to earth. There is another realm – the realm of heaven, God's kingdom – that has invaded fallen earth; we are to choose which side we are on. We are like the fighter in a confused guerrilla war who asked as mortar shells were falling, "Is that from our side or theirs?" The next fellow answered, "I don't know. Which side ya' on?" It is commanded us to be on God's side. Do we show it in every thought, word and deed? And *mean* it in our prayers – whatever that may cost us? We must remember that it is in the kingdom, and there only, that we will have joyous fellowship with our Lord, for that is where he is (John 14.2,3).

"Hallowed be thy name." In Jewish culture, and in the earliest Christian tradition, the name was always identified with the person. (This is true today in our culture, though it is not generally recognized.) Thus in honoring the name one honored the person. Consequently we are to revere the very name of God, never employ it casually or carelessly, but always accord it worship (worth-ship, as we saw in Chapter 2). Ours is an intensely personal God.

"Thy will be done." This is perhaps the most difficult for us of all the clauses in the Lord's prayer. Our natural tendency is to make up our minds what we want, or think is needed for ourselves and others, then ask God to ratify it by bringing his will to bear in its fulfillment. This is not the right approach. The meaning of the clause is that we are to surrender our will to God's will, as did Jesus (John 5.30). There must be for us but *one* petition: *thy* will be done. And if God's will is, today and always, *good*, what more can we desire or ask? The purpose of prayer is to bend *our* will to God's, not his to ours. In this the Christian way stands in stark contrast to all pagan religions, which seek in one way or another to manipulate God (or the "gods" as they imagine them) for the fulfillment of human desires.

We encounter then the little word *as*: "Thy will be done on earth *as* it is in heaven." It means, we will note repeatedly, *in the same way*. Again we put ourselves on the side of heaven. One might even say, "Thy will be done in this matter here on earth *in the same way* in which this matter is already being dealt with in heaven." Tito Colliander eloquently sums up the Orthodox understanding of all this, which is also the understanding of the early Church:

> When you pray, you yourself must be silent. You do not pray to have your own earthbound desires fulfilled, but you pray: Thy will be done. It is not fitting to wish to use God as an errand boy. You yourself must be silent; let the prayer speak [p. 65]. He who cannot make his will and hence his prayer coincide with God's will, will meet obstacles in his undertakings and constantly fall into the enemy's ambush. He becomes discontented or angry, unhappy, perplexed or impatient or troubled; and in such a state of mind no one can remain at prayer [p. 66] . . . external hindrance and opposition meet only the person who has not yielded his own will to God: and for God an obstacle is unthinkable [p. 22] . . . for a person with no wishes, everything goes just as he wishes . . . His will has coincided with God's will, and whatever he asks he will receive [pp. 34, 35].[1]

All this is difficult. It requires *self*-denial. It requires the trustfulness of love. But it shows us the Way of Life. And although we are to be silent and let God's will prevail, this does not mean that we just go all passive. On the contrary, prayer is *action*, as we have seen, and we are commanded to *persist*. We will return to this presently. First, let us finish the clauses of the Lord's prayer.

"Give us this day . . . " Jesus commands us to petition the Father for our day's needs. Who knows what tomorrow will bring? It is in our Father's hands. We are in exactly the position of the Israelites in Sinai when they depended on God for the daily manna that kept them physically alive. They were commanded to gather only what they needed for the day and not to keep any overnight (Exodus 16.19). But they did not listen to Moses, we are told, and what was kept overnight "bred worms and became foul," and Moses (who spoke for God) was angry with them (v.20). The incident prefigures Jesus' command. He specifically tells us that we are not to lay up stores for the future but to trust our Father day by day (Luke 12.32-34). He knows our needs better than we know our own. Whatever we keep beyond what the Father commands us will turn sour and become a burden to us.

"And forgive us our debts, as we have forgiven . . . " Here is another rough passage that becomes an obstacle for many of us, for most of us as we glibly recite this clause are not really aware of the implications of what we are saying. The problem is a limitation of our language displayed in the little word *as*. The words Jesus used meant *in the same way*, or even *in that precise degree to which* we forgive others. This is strong stuff, not at all the innocuous significance we habitually impute to the little word *as*. So, if we find ourselves not forgiven by God, or feel ourselves not forgiven, we have no legitimate complaint to Jesus. He can merely reply: "Did you, in asking forgiveness of the Father, at the same time forgive in the depths of your heart *all* who have ever offended you?" If not, our guilt remains. The forgiveness of our sins and offenses of all kinds, including the sins of the fathers that we mentioned earlier, is assured us by our Father *if we have fulfilled the condition of forgiving all that we have ever held against anyone else.* We are forgiven *in exactly that degree* to which we forgive others. In this is obedience and love.

So important is this command that we find it re-emphasized by Jesus in Mark 11.25: "And whenever you stand praying, forgive, if you have anything against any one; so that your Father also who is in heaven may forgive you your trespasses." And again in Luke 6.37: " . . . forgive, and you will be forgiven . . . " Jesus further drives home the point in the parable in Matthew 18 of the king who forgave his servants their debts (the "king" obviously standing for God, our Father) – but one servant refused to forgive another who owed money to *him*, and the king then wrathfully delivered the unforgiving servant to the jailers.

It is in forgiveness that we learn obedience and love. In fact, throughout our lives forgiveness will be the ultimate test of our obedience and love.

Finally, Jesus directs us to pray, " . . . lead us not into temptation, But deliver us from evil." Actually, the word translated *evil* in Matthew 6.13 might be more properly translated as *the evil one*. The early Church, and Orthodoxy today, knows nothing of an abstract evil, but only someone (spirit or person) *possessed of evil*, thus stressing the aspect of willful rebellion.

As Jesus' disciples, we are to leave it to the Father to manage our escape from situations of temptation and evil. Here we are brought up short once again. Are we not as Christians to fight temptation and evil? We are, but with a weapon that is sure and powerful, and that weapon is prayer – crying out to God. This is the opposite of what the "natural man"[2] within us desires. Natural man wants to prove his own strength. He tends to say to God, "Let me be tempted, test me, so that I can show what a strong Christian I am!" He wants to go out and do battle. But his strength to do battle is zero, and so also is the Christian's, but the Christian acknowledges his weakness and cries out to God, "Don't let me be tested like this! Rescue me from this evil!"

Thus did Jesus Christ command his disciples to pray. If we love him we will obey him in this, and keep at it, and at it, and at it . . .

We are Commanded to Persist

We mentioned earlier that the fact that God "does it all" does not mean that we are to sit back and go all limp and passive. On the contrary, we are to "pray without ceasing" (1 Thessalonians 5.17) – in a word, *work*. As with the violence that assures our obtaining the kingdom, persistence is required. *Sloth* is the enemy. Jesus commands, "Ask, and it will be given you; seek and you will find; knock and it will be opened to you" (Luke 11.9).

Ask . . . seek . . . knock . . . in prayer first, then move (or remain at rest), as God's spirit directs. But keep at it! This is so important that Jesus gives us two parables on persistence in prayer and the consequent assurance of its fullfillment. The first comes immediately following Luke's version of the Lord's prayer and just before the command to ask, seek, and knock:

> Which of you who has a friend will go to him at midnight and say to him, "Friend, lend me three loaves; for a friend of mine has arrived on a journey, and I have nothing to set before him"; and he will answer from within, "Do not bother me; the door is now shut, and my children are with me in bed; I cannot get up and give you anything"? I tell you, though he will not get up and give him anything because he is his friend, yet because of his importunity he will rise and give him whatever he needs (Luke 11.5-8).

The second, seven chapters later, has a touch of that dry humor so characteristic of our Lord:

> And he told them a parable, to the effect that they ought always to pray and not lose heart. He said, "In a certain city there was a judge who neither feared God nor regarded man; and there was a widow in that city who kept coming to him and saying, 'Vindicate me against my adversary'. For a while he refused; but afterward he said to himself, 'Though I neither fear God nor regard man, yet because this widow bothers me, I will vindicate her, or she will wear me out by her continual coming' " (Luke 18.1-5).

Our persistence is to be exactly like that of the widow. In just the four gospels, there are no less than thirty passages of commands, instruction, exhortation or example on persistence in prayer. We must take them seriously.

Do we love Jesus and desire to obey him? Then we'd better bend to the hard work of prayer. Prayer is not just for little old ladies with nothing better to do, though, bless them, they

do it. It is the highest calling of the most virile of men. Yet men
tend to leave it to women. Is it any wonder that our society has
gone soft? Set up a "prayer group" in almost any church, and
see how many men attend. They say they "don't know how
to pray." There are innumerable manuals on prayer. They don't
know because they have never really tried to find out. One leading Orthodox clergyman says that we should pray the Lord's
prayer thoughtfully at least seven times a day. That is an excellent way to begin.

Most men, of course, consider themselves hard-headed and
practical, and they want a guaranteed return for what they do.
Jesus himself guarantees God's answer to prayer. He said,
" . . . whatever you ask in prayer, believe that you receive it,
and you will" (Mark 11.24). And, " . . . if you ask anything of
the Father, he will give it to you in my name" (John 16.23). Can
there be any guarantee more sure than that?

Fasting

In the gospel of Matthew, immediately after the Lord's
prayer, Jesus instructs his disciples on fasting (Matthew 6.16-18).
Fasting was practiced by the Jews, and Jesus himself fasted (Matthew 4.2). Subsequently, after Jesus' ascension and the beginning of the Church, the disciples fasted (Acts 14.23).

This is not the place for an extensive discussion of fasting.
There are plenty of devotional manuals that tell how to fast,
and many churches have their own prescribed rules. The point
is that prayer and fasting go together (Mark 9.29). Jesus himself expected his disciples to fast after he had left them (Matthew 9.15). Fasting is an integral part of the Christian life.

Unfortunately, fasting today is little understood. It is seen
as a legalistic formality, not worthy of a person free in Christ.
And so it is, if seen merely as a legalism. Certainly it is ridiculous
to "fast" by throwing out leftover hash on Friday and going out
to buy lobster instead. But that is not at all what it means to
fast as a Christian.

To fast is to refuse to be self-indulgent. It is to refrain from
gossip, practice silence, put aside anger and lusts, and refuse

to be self-assertive. To deny oneself an extra, unneeded portion of any food is also to fast; to forego a much wanted dessert; to remain and comfort a friend who needs us, giving up a desired entertainment – all this is fasting. But to do it in self-pity or accompany it with self-congratulation ruins it, and it is not then fasting but an indulgence of the self under the pretence of a pious act. Even when we set ourselves a schedule of fasting, it is not the formality that counts, but the *intention.* Fasting is, in short, the self-denial that Jesus commands. It is an act of obedience and love.

What do we obtain in return? *Victory* in our struggle against the enemy! A famous monk of the seventh century wrote, " . . . the human race knew no victory before fasting . . . this weapon has deprived the devil of his strength . . . the sight of the weapon given us by our Supreme Leader burns him up. A man armed with the weapon of fasting is always afire with zeal."[3]

Tito Colliander notes that after Jesus fasted in the wilderness, angels came and ministered to him (Matthew 4.11), and adds: "They are waiting to minister to you, too."[4]

Notes

[1] Colliander, *The Way,* pages as noted.

[2] By "natural man" we mean man obeying his fallen nature. The early monastics would say that this is *un*natural man, because our proper "natural" state is to be as Adam was created, that is, not fallen, nor deified either, but a creature with potential for deification. An ironic twist to this came with Rousseau and the "Enlightenment" culminating in the French Revolution in the late eighteenth century. He and other secular philosophers of that time denied the Fall and postulated the "noble savage," uncontaminated by civilization – the very opposite of the Christian position. That the primitive person, untarnished by civilization, lives a joyful, innocent existence is demonstrably false, Rousseau and Margaret Mead notwithstanding. For the sake of clarity we will continue to use "natural man" in the contemporary Christian sense of obeying his earthly, fallen instincts.

[3] Isaac of Syria, *Early Fathers from the Philokalia,* p. 189.

[4] Colliander, *The Way,* p. 75.

B.
TO LOVE GOD IS
TO LOVE OURSELVES

Chapter Five

WE ARE FORGIVEN
AND HEALED

Jesus said, "You shall love your neighbor as yourself" (Mark 12.31). We are again up against that little word *as* that we discussed in the preceding chapter. It means, "in that precise degree to which." There is no doubt that we are meant to love our neighbor. Obviously we are meant also to love ourselves, but do we?

For many, Jesus' command means that we are to indulge our neighbor the way we like to indulge ourselves. But that is not at all what it means to love, as we saw in Chapter 2. Love is an act of will, of commitment, of obedience. It is kind, and strong. It "gives up cherished indulgences." It is *never self*-indulgent.

What, then does it mean to "love ourselves"? It means, precisely, to love ourselves *as God made us and intended us to be*. It emphatically does *not* mean that we are to love that state or condition of ourselves that we have arrived at through our own sinful foolishness. Would God be saying to Eve, "You are to love that desperate condition you are in as a result of having caved in to the serpent's beguilement?" Hardly. She is miserable; and Adam is miserable at having given in to her foolishness; then they both get tossed out of the Garden, and the whole human race has had to suffer the consequences – not in total depravity, for men were still able to recognize and respond to the goodness of God – but in the need for a divine savior.

The story of Adam and Eve has profound meaning for us. The truth it displays is at the very heart of our human condition. We are fallen from obedience; and fallen from obedience, we are fallen from grace and love, and our human condition is utterly wretched. Are we to love *this*? No.

But there remains in us that spark which knew Eden and loved it, and even now longs for it, for God was (and is) there. We desire to recover Eden, but of our own strength and effort we cannot do it. Therefore God sent his son to rescue us, and seeing in him the image of what we were and of what God means us to be, we can *love that image*, and in so doing love ourselves as God commanded. Jesus is *us* – as we were meant to be. That is why we are to love him. For in Christ is the coherence and balance of all things, including the coherence within ourselves that we desire. Without him is incoherence.

Our Loveless, Disobedient State

There is no possible way to understand this until we achieve a clear appreciation of our own loveless, sinful, fallen, disobedient condition, which is far worse than most of us realize, however miserable we may be. Only then can we begin fully to comprehend the immensity of what Jesus Christ did and has done, is doing and will do for us and all those who turn to him in submission and love.

Let us look around us, and at ourselves. It is not a pretty sight. What do we see? We see a pattern not of loving ourselves but of self-hate.[1] From this, and from the clamorous society that surrounds us, we seek in hundreds of ways, escape:

Escape first into *eros* and its perversion, lust. Indulgence of sensual passions to the utmost. This is advertised and promoted everywhere.

Alcohol and drugs.

Work. The workaholic is also an escapist. He can lose and forget himself in all that he is *doing* and feel virtuous about it. It is the perfect *self*-indulgence.

Orgies of anything. Bitterness about the past, about ourselves and what we have done, or failed to do, and bitterness toward others.

Cults. By letting ourselves be swallowed up in cultish beliefs or practices, or a cult community, we seek escape from the self we hate. Even the clergy, unfortunately, are not immune. There was a federal tax court case several years ago involving a mainline Protestant clergyman, who was also a chiropractor. He treated one of his women parishoners who was depressed and suicidal, without result, and billed her for it, then referred her to Scientology, one of the worst of the cults. Her husband sought to deduct the cost of her treatment as a medical expense, but the tax court denied it. The point of course is not the tax aspect (the court record merely serving to authenticate the facts of the case) but that here was a minister denying the power of his Lord, just as Saint Paul predicted (2 Timothy 3.5).

Indulgence in luxuries great and small, pleasures, possessions, clothes, travel, even busy-ness in "doing good" – anything, in fact, in excess that will help numb the conscience.

Armed aggression. Revolution. This also is indulgence, and escape. And again, the very elect are led stray. I shall never forget attending one Sunday in Southern California a beautiful Gothic church, one of the largest and wealthiest of a leading mainline Protestant denomination. They had a visiting minister who was billed as "the foremost ethical teacher of our time" conducting a weeklong seminar on "The Lifestyle of Truth," which was also the topic of his sermon that Sunday. He was quite blunt. The "lifestyle of truth" was revolution, and he meant with bombs and machine guns! The sedate, wealthy congregation made no move to throw him out of the pulpit, nor did they even seem shocked. Such is the climate of our time, and thus is Jesus' truth being perverted.

There is escape into physical disorders: neuroticism, hypochondria. Two seemingly opposite disorders that until recently were almost never seen but today are widespread are *anorexia nervosa* (a compulsive refusal to eat for fear of getting fat) and *bulimia* (a compulsion to eat, stuffing the stomach to where it can hold no more, then, often, throwing up and starting over again). In one recent Sunday issue of the Portland *Oregonian* there were two large ads by Portland area hospitals for their programs treating these "eating disorders." One even showed a teenage party ("Scarf and Barf" party) in which the "fun" was for everyone to eat up to the limit, vomit, then start over. There was a third large ad by a hospital for their program "especially for adolescents and their particular emotional or drug/ alcohol problems." A fourth large ad was by a prominent family for their missing teenage daughter who was "totally involved in rock music, punk style, new wave." The amount of self-hate in young people today has not begun to be measured, but the curve obviously is rising as the reservoir of love keeps dropping.

"Try anything." Tired of a specific escapist activity, some persons go "hog wild" indulging in anything they can. There is a popular series on TV in which a beautiful twenty-one-year-old actress is gang raped, has a lesbian affair, and commits incest with her brother. All this for viewing in the family living room! Our families are apparently desperate for the most far-out escapist "thrill" they can get, if not personally, then vicariously.

Homosexuality, fetishism, and all forms of sexual perversity reflect self-hatred. And there are other manifestations: arrogance, a studied selfishness, teasing, conceit, gossip, malicious imaginings, manipulations of others, flipness and "cuteness," seductive mannerisms, sadism, and child abuse. The list could go on and on.

"But," someone will say, "I'm not guilty of any of that. I'm just shacked up with my boy (or girl) friend, and we live a quiet life." Intimacy without commitment. This is not love. It is a recipe for disillusionment, sorrow and despair. It is contrary to all the catalogue of *agape* that we presented in Chapter 2. It is a parody even of *eros*. It won't do. God meant us to love ourselves *as he made us*. We are his creatures, and he so created us as to find love of ourselves and others only *in obedience to him*. Outside that obedience there is no love but at best only the pretence of love; at worst, hell, which is also "here and now" and "yet to come," as is heaven, whichever we will have.

We should note that virtually all of the patterns of self-hate that we have just listed also imply a hatred of others, or, at best, indifference to their true good and real needs – the opposite of *agape*. Indeed, a corollary of "thou shalt love thy neighbor as thyself" is "thou dost hate thy neighbor as thou hatest thyself." The specific commands of Jesus governing our relations to others we will discuss in Chapter 9.

Meanwhile, let us see what happens to us as we come into Jesus' presence, soiled and tarnished as we are by our failure to love ourselves as God commanded.

Healing Flows from Jesus' Divinity

Those who hate themselves are *sick*. This does not mean that any day now science will come up with a pill or a treatment that will cure self-hate. With the popularization in this century of psychology and psychiatry there has come a vogue for regarding even criminals as "sick," and therefore "curable" by medical means, but this has not worked, nor is it likely to, for as long as a person can *choose*, he is free to choose evil. Nevertheless, the word "sick" is appropriate, for reasons that will be apparent by the end of this chapter.

Jesus healed the sick. There is no record, in fact, that anyone who approached him with the desire and intent to be healed was not healed. It is also of a piece with our love and obedience to him, which includes recognition of *who he is*.

Jesus was preaching one day in the temple, and a furor arose among the Jews who were listening to him over exactly who he was. Jesus said to them, " . . . before Abraham was, I am" (John 8.58). *I am* here was the formula of the Jews for the divine existence. It meant *God*. But the word was so sacred the Jews never spoke it. So immediately they took up stones to throw at Jesus, but he hid himself and went out of the temple with his disciples. On their way, they passed a man blind from birth, and Jesus' disciples asked him, "Rabbi, who sinned, this man or his parents that he was born blind? Jesus answered, "It was not that this man sinned, or his parents, but that the works of God might be made manifest in him" (John 9.2,3).

The Jews, including Jesus' disciples, believed that sickness, including physical deformity, was a consequence of sin. Even today one might get that impression from a casual reading of the gospels. But in this instance Jesus denied that anyone sinned.

He then " . . . spat on the ground and made clay of the spittle and anointed the man's eyes with the clay, saying to him, 'Go, wash in the pool of Siloam' (which means Sent)" (vv. 6,7). The man did so, and came back seeing.

Either this is a "nice story" of Jesus' healing, which showed what a good and compassionate man he was, or it is something much more profound and significant. Let us consider the latter.

Just before Jesus makes clay with his spittle he utters his famous assertion: "I am the light of the world" (John 9.5). It is he, therefore, who gives light to the blind. Without him, we are all blind. Jesus applies the clay to the man's eyes. However, he still does not see. Jesus commands him to go wash in the pool that means "Sent." That is, he has to *act* in obedience to Jesus. There is the adumbration of baptism here, for completion of his passage into the New (restored) Life, which we will discuss in Chapter 10. Also, as we will see in Chapter 8, all of us after encountering Jesus are "sent." The man returns seeing; to us who have our sight, this can mean *understanding*. The man, incidentally, was a beggar. So are we all, until we have met Jesus. Then we enter his kingdom, which is filled with plenty.

Immediately after the man's return, there is a tremendous uproar. For one thing, the healing took place on the Sabbath and represented illegal "work." The Pharisees suspected some sort of hanky-panky and gave the man and his parents a bad time (is everything ever smooth for those who have proven in their own lives the authority of Jesus?), and they threw the man out of the temple. Then Jesus announced before the Pharisees that he had come to judge the world, "that those who do not see may see, and that those who see may become blind." Cryptic though this may sound to us, the Pharisees understood it. They had met their nemesis. Jesus was proclaiming a new order of things, for he was truly God, and they hated him for it.

The blind man trusted Jesus and obeyed him. He returned healed, and loved him, for out of obedience grows love. And loving him, he worshiped him (John 9.38). There is a subtle play on words in Jesus' telling the blind beggar to go to the pool called, "Sent," for Jesus said that he was himself "sent" from the Father (John 5.23). There is in fact a whole skein of significance in this story. Years could be devoted to unraveling the threads of meaning in just this one chapter of the gospel of John. For us at this point the main thing to note is that here Jesus has asserted his personal lordship over the conditions of men. This is why we love him, for only love can answer love, and the only response to absolute authority is obedience and worship. In the light of this we will understand the rest of our discussion of forgiveness and healing.

Our Action, Consent and Faith are Necessary

Possessing absolute authority from his Father, Jesus could presumably have passed through all the countryside simply commanding here, there and everywhere, "Be healed," and the sick would have been healed. But that is not the way God acts. Powerless though we are, he yet honors us by enlisting our cooperation, at least to the extent of asking our consent, for he treats as inviolable the free will with which he has endowed us. Almost every instance of Jesus' healing bears this out.

Jesus was one day in the synagogue, and there was a man with a withered hand, and it was again the Sabbath. Jesus commanded the man to come to him, and said, "Stretch out your hand" (Mark 3.5). The man obeyed and the hand was restored. The Pharisees were furious and "held counsel" how to destroy Jesus (Mark 3.6). Again, here was command and obedient action. The man was free to refuse to stretch out his hand and keep his deformity, though this would have undoubtedly saddened our Lord, just as the "hardness of heart" of the the officials saddened him. It is easy for us 2,000 years later to work up a passion of indignation against the Pharisees, but they were the acknowledged righteous ones of their time. Jesus was proclaiming his lordship of a new order of righteousness. Or, rather, it was to be the implementation of what God always intended, and had proclaimed through the Old Testament prophets. The sick and crippled acknowledged Jesus' lordship and were the first to benefit from it, for the "righteous" ones of the time could do nothing to heal them. This is an important theme, and terribly relevant for us today. We shall return to it presently.

Another instance of healing that instructs us about the new order of affairs takes place near the Sheep Gate in Jerusalem, where there was a pool called Bethzatha (or Bethesda), around which many invalids gathered. One man had lain there for thirty-eight years, and Jesus asked him if he wanted to be healed, then told him, "Rise, take up your pallet, and walk" (John 5.8), and the man did so. Later, Jesus finds him in the temple and tells him, "See, you are well! Sin no more, that nothing worse befall you" (John 5.14).

Again it was the Sabbath, so for the man to carry his pallet was a sin under Jewish law. In the eyes of officialdom, Jesus was *commanding* the man to sin! The man himself certainly understood this, but he obeyed Jesus, and, as a result, surely loved him for the healing he had been seeking for thirty-eight years. The man was putting behind him the suffering and misery he had endured so long and was about to enter the kingdom of which Jesus is Lord. What, then did Jesus mean by telling the man to "sin no more, that nothing worse befall you"? What could be worse than a crippling disease of thirty-eight years duration?

The answer is: to lose the kingdom, for which he had waited and suffered so long – having gotten that far, to blow it! Having been obedient, to become disobedient. The word translated "sin" in English means in Greek "to go wide of the mark," to aim at a goal and miss it. This applies to derelictions in obedience to God's law (we suffer for them) and to sickness, for we naturally aim at wholeness (health) and go wide of the mark. The "mark" is Christ. He is our health (wholeness); he is our righteousness. This is why one of the favorite passages of scripture among the early monastics was God's command in Deutronomy 5.32 to swerve "neither to the right nor to the left." The command to the cripple is aimed straight at us if we are to seek Jesus' kingdom in obedience and love.

There are three other gospels stories in which the message is very similar. Each involves the healing of a paralytic. The first in the ninth chapter of Matthew, tells simply that some people brought him a paralytic to be healed, and Jesus said to him, "Take heart, my son; your sins are forgiven" (Matthew 9.2). As usual, some Scribes were listening, and among themselves they accused Jesus of blasphemy, since only God can forgive sins. Jesus knew their thoughts and said, "Why do you think evil in your hearts?" By this he implied that *not to accept him for what he actually was* – that is, the son of God, – *was evil in itself.*[2] Then he asserts his authority to forgive sins and tells the paralytic to take up his bed and go home (Matthew 9.2-8).

The other two stories, one in the second chapter of Mark and the other in the fifth chapter of Luke, are the same, and differ only slightly from the one in Matthew. They tell of a paralytic let down through the roof of a house where Jesus was speaking because the press of the crowd was too great to get through. Jesus forgives his sins and tells him to take up his pallet and walk.

What are we to make of the significance of this for us today? If, humbly, we will think about it and truly examine our lives and actions, we will see that every one of us is a paralytic – incapable of constructive action, of love as God means us to love, unable to save ouurselves or do anything whatsoever worthwhile – until we come into the presence of Jesus and obey what he commands.

Jesus himself asserts this. He says, " . . . apart from me you can do nothing" (John 15.5). And Saint Paul adds, "I can do all things in him who strengthens me (Philippians 4.13).

There are those today who say that Jesus never asserted his divinity. They have simply not read the gospels. He asserted his divinity in everything he did. We are told in the seventh chapter of Luke that John the Baptist sent two of his disciples to Jesus to ask, "Are you he who is to come [meaning the messiah, the Christ, the son of God], or shall we look for another?" And Jesus tells them, "Go and tell John what you have seen and heard: the blind receive their sight, the lame walk, etc." In other words, what he is doing is the proof of his divinity. The effectual healing operation in each gospel instance seems almost incidential; it is merely the establishment of the prototype that is to be subsequently repeated throughout Christendom.

The point of Jesus' identity is crucial. One cannot be a Christian at all without acknowledging that Jesus is the son of God. His healing, however, was of a piece with his identity: it came from pity and love, love of such astounding depth that we cannot begin to fathom it. For he was, as the Nicene Creed asserts, of "one essence" with the Father, who is the source of all love, is indeed love itself. As the Son, Jesus had cosmic authority (John 5.27). The only viable response to *that* is submission, for if we refuse to submit and obey, then his commands hang permanently over us in judgment. Intolerable beneficence! We can bear it only because he is the sole source of what we most desire: *love*.

The Role of Faith

Total, unqualified belief in *who Jesus is* is summed up in one word: *faith*. We are now in a position to understand Jesus' use of the word in three final instances of healing:

There is a blind man by the roadside begging, near Jericho. Hearing a crowd passing, and learning that they are following Jesus, he cries out, "Jesus, Son of David, have mercy on me!" (Luke 18.38) Jesus commands that he be brought to him and asks what he wants. When he answers that he wants to receive his sight, Jesus says, "Receive your sight; your faith has made you well" (Luke 18.42). His faith is the efficient condition that made healing possible. The prayer of the blind man is the model of the "Jesus prayer," or "prayer of the heart," long used by contemplatives in the Orthodox tradition, except that they say, "Son of God" rather than "Son of David." With their keen spiritual insight, the early monastics would say that we are all of us blind (as well as being paralytics) until we have by faith had our eyes opened by Jesus Christ.

Matthew tells the story of Jesus moving in the midst of a crowd and of a woman having a chronic hemorrhage who secretly touched the edge of Jesus' garment and was healed. Jesus detected it and said, "Take heart, daughter; your faith has made you well" (Matthew 9.22).

Finally, there is the incident in Luke where Jesus is dining with Simon the Pharisee and a woman comes in and begins to weep and to anoint Jesus' feet with ointment and kiss them. Simon thought to himself that Jesus could be no prophet, otherwise he would have recognized the woman as a sinner. Jesus, however, turns to the woman and says, "Your faith has saved you; go in peace" (Luke 7.50). In other words, she worshiped him *because of who he was*. He then turns to Simon and makes a surprising connection between love and forgiveness, saying, " . . . I tell you, Simon, that her sins, many as they are, are forgiven; for she has shown me much love. But the man who has little to be forgiven has only a little love to give" (Luke 7.47).[3] Faith, as we can see from these examples, is not a lofty abstraction, but a *personal act of adherence, loyalty and obedience to Jesus Christ,* who is God.

We are now in a position to discuss those "sick" mentioned at the beginning of this chapter in the section, "Our Loveless, Disobedient State." We will discover something rather astounding – and in our day largely neglected.

Jesus, the Physician-Lover

Let us be utterly frank. We are Christians. Do we find ourselves continuously in the fellowship of Jesus Christ? Are we conscious of his holy presence in our lives from moment to moment? Do we constantly commune and converse with him? Do we feel his direction in our lives at all times?

To be honest, the answer is *no*. Perhaps intermittently we feel him guiding us. From time to time we sense his presence. But for long, long periods we are alone and on our own. Why?

Partly because he simply withdraws himself from time to time. He tests us, to see if we will be faithful even without his continuous presence. This has been the experience of the holiest of persons from the beginning. Sensing his absence, we will all the more desire his presence, and he desires to be desired. Also, he may withdraw so that we will become silent, for only in our silence can we hear him. In silence love meets love.

But there is another reason, and it is the major reason. It is also the reason why this present generation knows so little of Jesus Christ. We try to find him in the midst of clamor and confusion. We try to find him in idleness and comfort, in places of pleasure. We try to find him in our own synthetic happiness. But in none of these is he to be found. As a contemporary Orthodox teacher, Anthony Bloom, has pointed out, we cannot begin to find him until we silence the clamor within us and realize that we are standing *outside* his kingdom.

Where, then, is he? Let us listen to what he said. When the Pharisees asked why he ate with tax collectors and sinners, he said, "Those who are well have no need of a physician, but those who are sick" (Matthew 9.12). And again, "I came not to call the righteous, but sinners" (Mark 2.17). When in Nazareth he went to the synagogue and stood up to read, announcing the beginning of his ministry, he read from the 61st chapter of Isaiah: " . . . he [the Lord] has anointed me to preach good news to the poor. He has sent me to proclaim release to the captives [those in bondage to Satan] and recovering of sight to the blind [all of us], to set at liberty those who are oppressed [by the burden of religious legalisms], to proclaim the acceptable year of the Lord" (Luke 4.18,19). Jesus makes no secret of where he is. *He tells us plainly that he is with the poor, the afflicted, the broken-hearted, the sick, the suffering, the sorrowing, the dying, and those already dead — in sin.*

How often have we sat with a dying person, suffering with them, bearing the burden of their fear, truly sharing all that they are enduring? How often have we visited someone in prison, telling them they are loved, that someone cares about them? (If one cannot physically go there, it can be done with a letter — ask the chaplain to supply a name.) How often in our thought of Jesus have we seen him suffering, walked the tortured mile with him to Golgotha, wiped his brow and held his hand? Remember he said, " . . . as you did it to one of the least of these my brethren, you did it to me" (Matthew 25.40). If we have not done these things, and done them personally, as Jesus did, then we should not be surprised that we do not sense his presence. To spend billions in public moneys to "do good" may or may not produce some social and personal benefits, but of a certainty it does nothing to bring us into the presence of Jesus Christ.

We cannot, of course, personally do everything, but we must do at least what we can, starting with the person nearest us, our neighbor, as we will see in Chapter 9. *Then* we come close to Jesus, *then* we begin to love ourselves as he commanded us.

We can begin to understand now some curious anomalies. Some who are sick, handicapped, deformed, ugly seem more radiant with joy than we are. We long for the comfortable, pleasurable life. We would like to be among the jet set's "beautiful people," going here, there and everywhere, tasting the cream of everything, indulging every desire. Yet the "disadvantaged," as we euphemistically put it, are closer to Christ, if in humility they are accepting of their condition and love him still. Even Saint Paul endured a "thorn in the flesh," which God declined to remove (2 Corinthians 12.7). Yet Paul loved him none the less. And when the "beautiful people" renounce their indulgent life for the sake of Christ we are likely to see them so blessed that we become even more envious of them than before!

Thus when we ourselves become ill or sorrowful, miserable, deprived, suffering loss of everything we have, we should not think that we are "cursed by God." It can well be that he is permitting these things knowing that in them we will begin to acknowledge our own weakness and the corresponding power of Jesus Christ. We will then begin to love, adore, obey and worship him, and there discover the self that is truly us – the self that he commanded us love, instead of the sick, distorted indulgent self that we hate. Of one thing we may be certain: whatever our present condition – whether of radiant health or sickness and grief – when, ultimately, we go to meet our Lord it will be in suffering and sorrow. Death is not a pleasure trip.

True, Jesus could have healed everyone and set the whole world right at a stroke, abolishing hunger, pain, sorrow – every grief. He could also, when he was tempted, have made "stones into bread," thrown himself from the Temple without injury and wrested from Satan possession of the entire earth, setting up a benign government over all. And what would have happened to mankind? We'd have become a bunch of softies, romping and reveling in the goodness of God at no cost. God uses suffering. Through it he cauterizes the wounds of our sin. It is the route by which we enter into Christ's suffering and by which we are saved. *He chose* the way of suffering, so that, imitating him, we would grow in fortitude and discipline to be God's men and women.

Peter, a fisherman, an ordinary man, was plain, blunt, direct, caring about the truth, but sinful like us all (Luke 5.8) – a man we can feel with and understand. And he found his Lord – or, rather, his Lord found him, as in our hearts we also wish to be found. He has some advice for us:

> Since therefore Christ suffered in the flesh, arm yourselves with the same thought, for whoever has suffered in the flesh has ceased from sin [Jesus has come to us in our suffering to rescue us, as we noted above, and we have committed ourselves to him], so as to live for the rest of the time in the flesh no longer by human passions but by the will of God. Let the time that is past suffice for doing what the Gentiles like to do, living in licentiousness, passions, drunkenness, revels, carousing and lawless idolatry [the pagan Greeks were notorious for all this, and worse]. They are surprised that you do not now join them in the same wild profligacy, and they abuse you [sound familiar?]; but they will give account to him who is ready to judge the living and the dead [those engulfed in sin are already spiritually dead], that though judged in the flesh like men, they might live in the spirit like God (1 Peter 4.1-6).

But if, for the sake of obedience, and to receive Christ's love, we must endure sorrow and suffering, there are rewards for our sacrifice, as we will see in the next chapter.

Notes

[1] To love ourselves as God intended us is the very opposite of the "self-love" of which we will be speaking repeatedly later on. That "self-love" is self-worship, the substitution of the worship of man for worship of God; as such, it amounts to self-hate.

[2] Someone will immediately raise the question, "Then how do you account for the success of scientists who do not believe in God?" I would answer that the scientist is concerned with *truth*, and Jesus said, "*I* am the way and the truth . . . " (John 14.6). Truth is its own authority and its own success. The scientist, *as scientist*, is in his desire for truth closer to God than he suspects.

[3] J. B. Phillips, *The New Testament in Modern English* (New York, 19 60). Hereinafter designated *P.*

Chapter Six

OUR NEEDS ARE SUPPLIED

The process of forgiveness and healing which God sent his son to effect in us is meant, as we have seen, to restore us to that original image of himself that God intended us to be. *Then we will be able to love ourselves and others as God meant us to love.* God in Christ is indeed doing a "new thing" (Isaiah 43.19; Revelation 21.5).

To understand the new, however, we have to remind ourselves of the old. The old was our condition of fallenness, and it is still with us — we live in two worlds, the fallen and the redeemed, and our goal is to fill our lives with the latter, permanently. The story of Adam and Eve, so profound in its meaning, bears constant remembering. Once, in our total dependence upon God, we are in bliss. With our disobedience to God, enmity entered; love for God and for our fellows was replaced with hate or indifference. And we were punished. God said to Adam: " . . . cursed is the ground because of you; in toil you shall eat of it all the days of your life; . . . In the sweat of your face you shall eat bread . . . " (Genesis 3.17,19). *Our needs, our daily bread, are to be supplied through our own toil and sweat.*

It is a difficult habit to break. We continue to toil, sweat and struggle. But God, loving us so much that he "gave his only begotten son" to redeem us ("buy us back") from our fallen and (mistakenly) self-reliant state, is not only going to forgive our sins and heal us, but *provide for all our needs* as we submit to him in love and work with him in obedience.

There is a real whammy in this. We have begun to learn

what it means to live the commands of Jesus: we grow in loving him, and in loving and obeying him we receive healing and forgiveness; we even receive, as we have seen, the kingdom of heaven here and now! *This is great,* we say. But are we ready for the next thing that is required of us?

The next thing required is that we are to trust him absolutely with respect to all our needs, money and possessions. This will be a real test of our love, trust and obedience.

We are Not to Strive for Material Things

After the urgency with which Jesus commands us to follow him, to seek the kingdom, and to pray, it is a shock to find him casual, off-handed, even negative, about those things of greatest concern to our natural selves: needs, money and possessions. Look at these commands:

"Do not labor for food which perishes . . . " (John 6.27).

"Do not lay up for yourselves treasures on earth . . . " (Matthew 6.19).

" . . . whoever of you does not renounce all that he has cannot be my disciple . . . " (Luke 14.33).

" . . . do not be anxious about . . . what you shall eat . . . drink . . . put on . . . (Matthew 6.25).

" . . . do not be anxious about tomorrow . . . " (Matthew 6.34).

"You received without pay, give without pay" (Matthew 10.8).

That God, through his son, should make himself responsible for *all* our needs should not really surprise us. As Saint Paul wrote, "He who did not spare his own Son but gave him up for us all, will he not also give us all things with him?" (Romans 8.32).

When he established the "new covenant" in the person of Jesus, God rescinded the punishment he laid on Adam. Someone will immediately object that we still have to struggle and grub! So we do; as we said, we still live in *two* worlds. But do we have to be as determined about it as most of us are? Why not try prayer, submitting ourselves to the commands and manner of praying that we studied in Chapter 4? For Jesus commanded:

"Ask, and it will be given you . . . " (Luke 11.9).

And, to be honest, has not material prosperity on earth increased since the coming of Christ? And should we not in honesty attribute it more to God's mercy and love than to our own strength and cleverness? In the Christian era now passing, many loved and were obedient; many prayed, sought the truth and were humble. Are we to say that this was totally unrelated to the outpouring of material benefits we have received? By the time we put that theory to a "scientific" test, it may be too late, and out of humility compelled by ruination all about us we may have to start all over again in trust, obedience and prayer. Best we hold on to the achievements granted us.

The first of the scripture quotations that we cited in this section follows just after the account of the feeding of the 5,000. The crowd had come along after Jesus, and he told them they were doing it "because you ate your fill of the loaves" (John 6.26). He was telling them they were of the type later known to missionaries as "rice Christians." They followed whoever would give them a handout. Jesus then tells them, "Do not labor for the food which perishes, but for the food which endures to eternal life, which the Son of man will give you; for on him has God the Father set his seal" (John 6.27). Immediately they want to know what, then, they should labor for, and Jesus tells them, "This is the work of God, that you believe in him who he has sent" (v. 29). They get into more hot discussions of what this means, and Jesus then silences them with the prodigious affirmation (v. 41): *"I am the bread which came down from heaven."* And again (v. 48): *"I am the bread of life."* Jesus continues, then, setting forth the meaning of the sacramental partaking of his flesh and blood in holy communion, the Eucharist, which we will discuss in Chapter 10. The issue here is clearcut. It is a matter of *who Jesus is.* Those who did believe were thereafter to follow him in obedience and love, trusting him for everything.

We are dealing now with commands that touch us where we are most hard-headed and stubborn. Of all Jesus' commands, these may be the most difficult for us. What, then, are we to do? We begin by giving up, by surrendering the clutter in our lives, so there will be room for God to move around and give us what we really need.

We are Not to Hoard

Immediately after instructing his disciples in how to pray, giving them the Lord's Prayer, and in how to fast, Jesus tells them, "Do not lay up for yourselves treasures on earth, where moth and rust consume and where thieves break in and steal, but lay up for yourselves treasures in heaven . . . For where your treasure is, there will your heart be also" (Matthew 6.19-21).

Consider this a moment. Our time on earth is short. When we are twenty, we think it will be forever. By the time we are seventy (and those fifty years whisk by in a wink), we *know* it is short. In the meantime we have accumulated junk by the ton: bric-a-brac, albums of photos, rugs, chinaware, a far larger house than we can use – property of every sort. Now we try to begin getting rid of it; it's ten times harder than we think it will be. If it were just an intellectual matter, we could toss it away easily; but the stuff has got a grip on our hearts, and we find ourselves concocting a hundred reasons why each thing cannot be disposed of – after all, we may *need* it (we think). We won't. The only thing to do is obey Jesus and get rid of it. Then our hearts will automatically go out to Jesus and to the spiritual riches that are the true wealth which only he can give us. One of the great Christian writers of this century, Charles Williams, has said we are much more disposed to believe that Jesus was right about the heavenly mysteries than that he was merely accurate about the facts of everyday life.[1] But if we are inclined not to believe that Jesus knew what he was talking about when he spoke of corruption (rotting, rusting, cobwebbing, disintegration) of material things, all we have to do is take a look in our attic, basement, barn and less-used closets. Ugh! The word is: *out with the garbage*; either give it to charity, or sell it and give the proceeds. For improving the spiritual climate, there is nothing like a good big garage sale, provided *everything goes*.

In Mark and Luke there are parallel passages to the one in

Matthew. The one in Mark 10.17-22 is one of the most moving in the New Testament. An attractive young man, rich, good-looking probably, and *spiritually concerned*, runs up to Jesus and *kneels before him,* asking what he must do to inherit eternal life. The guy had everything going for him, *everything* — looks, money, and a desire for God. And Jesus, we are told, "looking upon him, loved him . . . " (Mark 10.21). How many of us today would not give everything to be in that fellow's sandals? And he blew it. Here was failure of love and obedience. For Jesus told the young man to dispose of all his wealth to the poor, then follow him. But he went away "sorrowful." He failed to obey. Love did not answer love.

Finally, in Luke 12.32-34 Jesus tells us his disciples with the utmost tenderness, "Fear not, little flock, for it is the Father's good pleasure to give you the kingdom," then goes on to tell them that the condition is to get rid of their possessions.

We have not in this section dealt with the heroic example of many of the great ones of the kingdom, such as Saint Francis and the early ascetics who truly gave up everything and even forgot to eat for days at a time. For most of us today, a heroic garage sale may be all we can manage. But let that be just a beginning; as in peeling an onion, we have to shuck our possessions layer by layer, and as we do that we will become increasingly aware of the profound significance of what Jesus was saying about treasures, and we will come closer and closer to the "pearl of great price" that in our hearts we most desire.

But We Must Count the Cost

If we are still somewhat appalled at the prospect of what we are to give up, there is worse to come. In Luke 14 Jesus tells his disciples to calculate the cost of following him. He notes that if we are going to construct a building we first sit down and count the cost; otherwise, after building the foundation we may find we don't have the resources to complete it, and so become the object of ridicule. Or, he says, we should be like a king going to war; he first calculates if he has enough men to defeat his enemy. Jesus then shows us what the bill is going to be for according him absolute obedience and love: "So therefore, whoever of you does not renounce all that he has cannot be my disciple" (Luke 14.33).

This is tough teaching. It reads beautifully in the pulpit on Sunday morning when everyone is comfortable and well dressed. Christianity is *so* idealistic, isn't it? But that is exactly what it is *not*, as we noted in Chapter 1. It is hard reality. Jesus meant what he said. But immediately we are given reassurance. Jesus tells us, " . . . do not be anxious about your life, what you shall eat or what you shall drink, nor about your body, what you shall put on" (Matthew 6.25). This is followed by a long discourse on the Father's provision for all of our needs. The same discourse occurs in Luke 12. These are, unfortunately, passages that have become almost too familiar through repetition; we tend not to take them seriously. But to one hearing them for the first time they are an astonishment. This Christian God supplies *everything*? So he does. Jesus said, "And why are you anxious about clothing? Consider the lilies of the field, how they grow; they neither toil nor spin; yet I tell you, even Solomon in all his glory was not arrayed like one of these" (Matthew 6.28,29). On the face of it, this verges on satire. Woe to the man who quotes it to his wife when she says she has nothing to wear! But our Lord was simply emphatic. We must get rid of all that we can do without – or, better, all that God does not tell us to keep. Then we will get our priorities (values) straight. Once we do that, *things do work out*, as countless Christians have testified. Anxiety is no help but an enemy.

Jesus acknowledges that there will be "those days" when everything goes wrong and we become fearful of the future. But he tells us we are to take heart: "Therefore do not be anxious about tomorrow, for tomorrow will be anxious for itself. Let the day's own trouble [adversity, misfortune] be sufficient for the day (Matthew 6.34). In Basic English it is rendered even more simply: "Then have no care for tomorrow: tomorrow will take care of itself. Take the trouble of the day as it comes." Events and concerns that impinge on us are mostly outside our control. But we can limit our concerns about them and safely commit them to God, who will reward us: "Weeping may endure for a night, but joy cometh in the morning" (Psalms 30.5 *KJV*).

There are other commands of Jesus concerning possessions, such as: " . . . sell what you possess and give to the poor . . . " (Matthew 19.21); "Take heed, and beware of all covetousness; for a man's life does not consist in the abundance of his possessions" (Luke 12.15). And so on. There is, in fact, so much in all the New Testament admonishing against concern with earthly wealth that it is easy to belabor the subject. There is no such emphasis in the Old Testament, where in fact wealth was taken as a mark of righteousness. The new attitude toward wealth is to be a signal feature of the new life in Christ. If we are to love and obey him, we must adopt that attitude.

In Obedience, We Cast Our Nets

So what are we to do? Are we to sell the car, house and furniture and take the wife and kids and go live in a cave? No. That is to mock what Jesus meant.

It is a matter of our orientation – where are values and priorities lie. It can mean getting rid of a great deal, the TV perhaps first, because we tend to worship it. Whatever it is that contradicts the kingdom, or is an obstacle to it, must go. We must apply intelligence and discernment. It will also take a strong will. This is undoubtedly what Jesus meant when he said, " . . . it is easier for a camel to go through the eye of a needle than for a rich man to enter the kingdom of God" (Matthew 19.24). And to accomplish it, we must ask for divine help, for Jesus added, "With men this is impossible, but with God all things are possible" (v. 26).

Then miracles begin to happen. Jesus tells us, " . . . set your heart on his [the Father's] kingdom, and your food and drink will come as a matter of course" (Luke 12.31,*P*).

When Jesus first met Peter by the lake of Gennesaret he commanded him, "Put out into the deep and let down your nets for a catch" (Luke 5.4). Peter protested that they had fished all night and caught nothing, but he obeyed, and the catch was so huge that they "filled both boats, so that they began to sink" (v. 7). There is a profound symbolism here. If we obey Jesus in trust and love, we have indeed "put out into the deep." We also have to *act* in obedience (put down our nets). We obey after a time of dearth in our lives (fished all night and caught nothing), and we are overwhelmed by the harvest. There is even a double significance in this, for immediately after the great catch of fish Jesus says to Peter: "Do not be afraid; henceforth you will be catching men" (v. 10). We will discuss this in Chapter 8.

Do we begin to get the knack of this? Here is the lesson: 1) We pare possessions to the minimum. 2) We refrain from getting grabby for anything, either tangible or intangible (whether physically or in our imagination it's the same), and let the other fellow be first. 3) We refrain from striving beyond what God requires of us, but *let him give to us*, for what he gives will be far better than anything we can obtain for ourselves. 4) *Then* we will be ready for the mission Christ commands us of bringing others to himself.

Meanwhile, in our fallen state, which has weakened us, there is an ogre that looms over us: *fear*. If we are to love ourselves as God intends us, we cannot live with fear. We proceed now to what Jesus commands us about fear.

Notes

[1] Charles Williams, *He Came Down from Heaven* (London, 1950), p. 89.

Chapter Seven

WE FEAR GOD
– AND FEAR NOT

There are times, we must admit, when fear seizes us by the throat and we are all but paralyzed. Someone close to us is ill, and we care terribly, and fear what may happen. Death looms for us or for someone very dear to us, and we are horribly frightened. We lose our job, and how will we live? War threatens, and a son or husband may be called up. Or a son or daughter may get into drugs or delinquency, and we tremble before the prospect of a ruined life. Fear gnaws at us, and we try to escape, but we find no escape. A blase spirit is nothing but a posture and a cover-up, and we know it, for underneath it we can feel the fear continuing to work its insidious depredations.

Yet in this book we are studying obedience and love, and John, the beloved disciple, writes: "There is no fear in love, but perfect love casts out fear. For fear has to do with punishment, and he who fears is not perfected in love" (1 John 4.18). ("Perfect" and "perfected" here have the sense of something fully realized, completely developed, no longer partial but total.) Either the Apostles knew and practiced something we do not have, or else they led a charmed life. But a charmed life is exactly what they did not lead. Sorrow, suffering, persecutions were their daily lot – yet they did not fear, but simply loved. If we also are to love as Christ commanded us, which includes loving ourselves, we must learn to put away fear.

Two Kinds of Fear

To begin to understand fear and how Jesus removed his disciples' fears, and will also remove ours, we need first to distinguish at least two kinds of fear.

The first may be called existential[1] fear. It is inherent in our fallen human situation. It includes "guilty fear," which is the dread experienced by us all because we have transgressed against the "rightness" of things as God created them. We know in our hearts that we will have to answer for these transgressions. The second is the awe or dread of a power greater than ourselves which we are drawn to respect at least, and even to worship and adore, as were the witnesses to Jesus' transfiguration, which we will discuss presently.

As for the existential, we fear because:

1) *We are going to die.* For all the progress in medicine, the mortality rate of all creatures remains at 100%, and there is no earthly prospect of reducing it, ever.

2) *We are under judgment.* There is no man alive but in his innermost being knows that sooner or later he must give an account of what he has done for good or for ill, and suffer the consequences. This is conscience, and no one is ever without it, however deadened it may be temporarily.

3) *Our human condition is uncertain.* Most of the events that impinge on our daily lives are beyond our control (who knows what the next telephone call may bring?); we are thus at the mercy of events, and we cannot know whether those events will be beneficent or harmful.

4) Finally, *we are mired in entropy.*[2] In this earthly existence, the second law of thermodynamics operates relentlessly. It is the law not of change only, but of change inexorably proceeding in the direction of decay, dissolution, loss and destruction, annihilation. It happens to everything. Whatever is painstakingly, even gloriously constructed or formulated will eventually fall apart. It was Christ and Christ only who could say, "Heaven and earth will pass away, but my words will not pass away" (Luke 21.33). And it was Christ and Christ only who by his resurrection reversed entropy for the first and only time in history.

All this generates uncertainty and misgivings in us, and

provokes fear. But God did not mean it to be so. He set Adam and Eve[3] in a garden with everything provided for them, on one condition: *obedience*. But Adam and Eve decided to go it on their own. Pride (*hubris*) rose up in them. They disobeyed, and fear entered. Adam's first words after the fall were, "*I was afraid*" (Genesis 3.10), for disobedience casts out love and introduces fear. And so it has been with us ever since – until the coming of Christ. Even then, the renewal of love and obedience in a right relationship to God is not automatic, for just as Adam and Eve *chose* to disobey, so we must *choose* our salvation in Christ, choose to act according to his instructions, and (ghastly thought though it is), he leaves us free to reject him and to refuse to act.

Jesus Commands us: "Fear Not!"

In our human situation of endemic fear, Jesus gives us specific commands. We need again to remember that Jesus never discoursed speculatively or philosophically, but simply commanded us what to do. And his commands are practical, for he spoke in "real life" situations.

Jesus is speaking to his disciples about people's attitude toward him and what it will be toward them. He has just spoken of his vilification by his own people, who have called him Beelzebul[4], and he warns his disciples they will be even more maligned than he is. So, foreseeing martyrdom for his followers, he commands them, "And do not fear those who kill the body but cannot kill the soul . . . " (Matthew 10.28; we will deal with the rest of the verse a little later on.) Immediately, then, comes his tender reassurance that not a sparrow falls without the Father's will and that "even the hairs on your head are all numbered [known]" (v. 30). And so he commands, "Fear not, therefore; you are of more value than many sparrows" (v. 31). This command is meant to have for us in these latter days all the force and comfort that it had for Jesus' immediate hearers, and we can well use it, for our times are fully as hostile to the faith as they were then, as we shall see in a later chapter.

We mentioned earlier that we fear an awesome power

greater than ourselves. It is not surprising, therefore, that Jesus'
transfiguration occasioned fear on the part of the disciples. The
Feast of the Transfiguration is observed in Roman Catholicism
and Orthodoxy as one of the greatest of holy days, but in Prot-
estantism it is largely neglected. It is celebrated on August 6,
which is also the day we dropped the first atomic bomb (Hiro-
shima), a coincidence that is not without humiliating significance
for us in showing the contrast between Christ's glory, which he
would share with us if we would have it, and our lethal contri-
vances with which we presume to control destiny.

Next to the resurrection, the transfiguration is the greatest
of the mystical events in Jesus' earthly life. In the midst of it
Peter is speaking to Jesus when the voice of God cuts him off
with, "This is my beloved Son, with whom I am well pleased;
listen to him" (Matthew 17.5). The instant reaction of the three
disciples who were present (Peter, James and John) was exactly what ours probably would have been: stunned terror. They
fell flat on their faces. We are simply not equipped to encounter God directly without terror. Jesus instantly came and touched
them, then told them to rise and have no fear.

The transfiguration scene, which is one of the most moving
in the four gospels, has some subtle and far-reaching lessons:

1) It specifically confirms that Jesus is the Son of God.

2) Jesus *touched* them. As an act of reassurance, this
was undoubtedly effective, but it is also symbolic. We should
picture the scene and reflect on it. He who had just been
acknowledged by God as his son immediately touched the
sons of men, showing himself the mediator between God
and men, and conferring upon men who accepted him as
God's son the right and ability to stand without terror before almighty God himself.

3) He *spoke*, telling the disciples to rise and have no
fear. Fear of what? The presumption is that they are not
to fear that they would be rejected by God; not to fear that
in their unworthiness they could not be made worthy; not
to fear that the mediation of Jesus between God and man

would be insufficient to save them.

4) Finally, a lesson for us here and now is that, believing the transfiguration, we also are to be witnesses to it and proclaim the divinity of Jesus.[5]

Another moving and very human scene is given us in Mark 5. Jairus, a synagogue official whose daughter is dying, asks Jesus to come and lay hands on her and save her life. Jesus accepts, and while they are going to his house, someone from the household comes to tell Jairus that his daughter has died, so there is no need to trouble Jesus further. Jesus overhears this and immediately says to Jairus, "Do not fear, only believe" (Mark 5.36). All of us are naturally fearful in the face of death, but here is Jesus telling Jairus not to fear. Then he goes and restores the girl to life. The command is to us as well, and from it we learn:

1) Jesus is not put off by death. He had overcome it. Death has no authority over him, for he is the conqueror of death and the Lord of Life and the God of our resurrection. As an ancient phrase sung repeatedly in Orthodox churches during the Easter season has it: "He has trampled down death by [his own] death."

2) Fear negates faith and love, without which there is no restoration of life.

3) Believing in the power of Jesus makes possible his act of restoration. It is of course presumptuous to assert that his power is limited; still, we are reminded that our consent and belief are necessary – he could perform no miracles in Nazareth because his fellow townspeople did not believe in him (Luke 4.24).

Finally, there is the scene at the Last Supper when Judas has just departed to carry out his betrayal. Jesus prophesies that before dawn Peter will deny him three times. One can imagine the ensuing scene: exclamations, mutterings, confusion, uproar. Jesus immediately calms them, saying, "Let not your hearts be troubled [don't be afraid]; believe in God, believe also in me." That command is meant for us all *right now*, as we look around

and see Jesus being betrayed on every side, even by those presumed to be most loyal to him, and become deeply disturbed
and fearful. Jesus and his Father are going to set things right in
their own time and in their own way; they are about to create the
new "logic" of a Way of Life *through death and resurrection*.
This is the "new thing" proclaimed by the prophet (Isaiah 43.19).
It is a thing that does not in the least conform to the pagan Greek
logic of material things. Rather, it is the life given us by God,
which goes far beyond restoring the bliss of Eden but takes us into
heaven itself, the very kingdom of God! When God says to us,
"Fear not . . . " as the Angel Gabriel said to Mary (Luke 1.30 KJV),
our response must be to obey and love, as she did: "Behold
the handmaid [servant] of the Lord; be it unto me according
to thy word" (Luke 1.38 KJV).

There is One to be Feared

Jesus' commands to us concerning our fears are wonder-
fully reassuring. No longer are we impelled to hide, as was Adam
after the disobedience, and say, "I was afraid," because God
has forgiven our disobedience – if we will but obey his Son, in
love. We are not even to fear the persecutions that will come
upon us as a consequence of that love and obedience. We saw
this in the first command concerning fear in Matthew 10.28.
But now we come to deal with the rest of v. 28, and it is a stunning command.

The command reads, " . . . *fear him who can destroy both
soul and body in hell*."

If indeed there is someone, or something, to fear, we had
better take note. Who is the "him" in this command? Our first
reaction probably is, "Why Satan, of course, the old temptor
and deceiver. Who else?" But it is not. It is the selfsame God
the Father whom Jesus immediately portrays as loving us with
such great tenderness that he knows how many hairs are on
our head and counts us as of more value than all the sparrows
in creation!

We had better pay attention here, for we are confronting
one of the great radical truths of the gospel, namely that God's

tender love for us is of a piece with his wrath and the finality of his terrible judgment. Kenneth S. Wuest in a full, literal translation of the original Greek renders the passage as follows: " . . . be fearing him who has the power to bring both soul and body to the condition of utter ruin and everlasting misery in hell."[6] The corresponding passage in Luke 12.5 is no less severe. Wuest renders it: "But I warn you whom to fear. Fear the one who, after he kills, has the authority to throw into hell."

How is it that he who is love itself, who cares more for us than we care about ourselves, can willingly cast us into hell? The answer is, "not willingly," for it is not his will that "any should perish" (2 Peter 3.9). On the other hand, he is Creator, Father, Judge. All the circumstances and conditions of our being were established by him, and one of them is free will. In and through his Son, Jesus Christ, he has instructed us in the way that finds favor with him. He has given us a way to avoid condemnation. As Peter said to Jesus, "You have the words of eternal life" (John 6.68). He has also instructed us not only by word and example but by giving us a conscience. The way of salvation is open to us. God is not a capricious judge, but has made his terms absolutely clear. So the game is fair: *we are free to choose.* And if destruction is our choice, then destruction we assuredly will have. In his novel *The Great Divorce* C. S. Lewis, quoting George MacDonald in "heaven," has him saying, "There are only two kinds of people in the end: those who say to God, 'Thy will be done', and those to whom God says, in the end, '*Thy* will be done.' All that are in Hell, choose it. Without that self-choice there could be no Hell. No soul that seriously and constantly desires joy will ever miss it. Those who seek find. To those who knock it is opened."[7]

"But," we cry out, "what if Satan *compels* us?" To which the answer is that Satan has no power to compel anyone, nor to cast soul and body into hell if we (or others on our behalf) call upon God to save us. Satan can only seduce, and his seduction can be successful only by our consent. In our hands is the tragic power to accept, or to refuse, our salvation.

In these days of "positive thinking" the issue of hell and salvation is being neglected. Some preachers tell us that indeed
all will be saved — without bearing the cross of God's judgment.
This is a doctrine of "cheap grace," and it is a false doctrine,
for there is no such grace. We must all bear the cross of Christ.
We have today a reaction to the "hell fire and damnation"
preaching of an earlier generation, but the fiery preachers had
a point, however much they may have failed to balance it with
the message of God's caring and love. The number of persons
frightened into good behavior and respect for God simply out
of obedience to Jesus' command, *"Fear him!"* is perhaps incal-
culable.

*   *   *   *   *

We need to pause here and reconcile clearly in our minds
Jesus' commands to "fear not" with his unequivocal command
to "fear God." It is not difficult if we will think in terms of the
realities of our human condition and the realities of God as set
forth in the Bible, instead of in terms of our own bright philosophical ideas.

In the first place, the condition of fallen Adam ("I was afraid"),
which we share with him, is now remedied. After the reassurance
Jesus gave his disciples at his transfiguration, we do not need
to hide from God. We do not need in fact to fear even death
itself, for Jesus, as we saw, is victorious over death. We are
invited into the very heaven of God! So if we continue in our
fears we are hurting ourselves, certainly not loving ourselves
as we are commanded, *and* are refusing heaven! Earthly fears
can be stultifying, numbing our faith, paralyzing our will to believe. This is why Jesus said to Jairus, "Do not fear, only believe."
He was saying in effect, "I am here, *I* can handle this matter."
He says precisely that in *every circumstance* to all of us who
turn to him today.

Our fears unfortunately however do not just glide away by
our wishing it. Like soiled tissues, they have to be thrown
somewhere. Where? Onto Christ. As Peter says, "Cast all your

anxieties on him . . . " (1 Peter 5.7). And so we can, for Jesus said, " . . . I am with you always . . . " (Matthew 28.20).

As for our fear of God, the central reality is his *almightiness.* In the face of that, we are naturally to fear, as Christ commanded. After all, do we really desire a God who is *not* almighty? No. But then does this not introduce the dread and terror that are the very negation of love? And are we not commanded to love God with all our heart and soul and mind? No, it does not negate love. For in love that is real and deep there is always an element of fear. Ask any bridegroom. When he takes his bride to the altar, if there is not element of awesome fear and wonder at the responsibility he is taking on, at the enormity of what he is doing, then it is safe to say there is not much love, that the marriage is probably based on superficial desires or convenience rather than on the joyous mystery of profound spiritual and physical union.[8]

Difficult as these matters may be for us, superficiality being the dominant mode of our time, they were studied deeply by the Church's early monastic teachers, who understood them perfectly. One of them writes, " . . . the greater our longing for God, the greater grows our fear; and the more we hope to attain God, the more we fear him."[9] And another: "Fear of God purifies us through awe and self-abasement. . . . Without fear we cannot acquire intense love for the divine . . . "[10]

There is one final thought we may reflect on here in connection with Jesus' commands. If someone gives us an unconditional command, and we obey it, then that person who gave the command *is responsible for the consequences.* Conversely, if we do not obey, then that person is absolved of responsibility and we bear it ourselves. If our doctor says to take such and such medicine according to a certain schedule and we obey, he has taken the responsibility for curing us, but if we ignore his directive we have no one else to blame but ourselves when our sickness continues. Jesus is the physician who has come to us and given us commands; if we obey his commands, then we have victory over the whole range of our ills, including death itself. He is in himself the "new Adam." Must we not then surely love him just as he loves us?

Even so, whenever we permit the old Adam to return in us with his self-sufficient pride (*hubris*) and disobedience, then our fear returns.

Fear of Christ

That pride, that *hubris*, is our human disease. It is what caused Adam to assert himself against God. Like a drowning man who is thrown a lifeline and refuses it, we would rather preserve a false independence against a sure salvation. We would rather live with a faint hope of saving ourselves than surrender ourselves in obedience to the love Christ offers. We fear Christ himself, because of what he requires of us.

Men also stand in awe and dread of Christ because they know his power. He *can* compel — but will not. We must therefore surrender voluntarily, disclosing before God the nakedness which Adam and Eve tried to conceal. We must:

Lay our shame before God.

Become lowly, accepting to be carried through life on nothing more exalted than a donkey, as was Jesus.

Accept the wounds to our self-love (the *self*-centeredness that asserts itself against the "otherness" of God), that result from self-surrender.

Learn to suffer and be silent.

Lay aside all impatient concern about the future.

Refuse to pity ourselves (a form of self-love).

Stop trying to please men, but try to please only God.

Refuse to give up, knowing that the greater the grace and love given us by God, the greater will be our trials and temptations.

Be willing to become the least, instead of the first, and forego that harsh, critical "goodness" that is against the spirit of Christ.

Stop being "eager," but await God's quiet grace and become obedient to it.

Renounce our own will and trust nothing in our own strength.

In all that we do or think, live constantly in the presence of God.

This is but a short list, to give us an inkling of what is required. And what do we get in return? An end to *all* our fears! At the beginning of this chapter we listed four circumstances of our human condition that generate in us existential fears. We are now in a position to see how the love of God for us in and through Jesus Christ obviates all these fears:

1) *We are going to die.* But God in Christ has given us eternal life (John 10.28). He has "trampled down death by death." Physical death is no longer final but a mere incident in eternity.

2) *We are under judgment.* Yes, but if we confess our sin and accept God's judgment, we are immediately forgiven. (1 John 1.9).

3) *Our human condition is uncertain.* Yes, but not to God in Christ, who "knows everything" (John 21.17); thus we are, as we saw, to "cast all our anxieties on him."

4) *We are mired in entropy.* So we are. But once, and once only, in all history was entropy reversed, and that was in the resurrection of Jesus from the dead, in whose resurrection we participate (Romans 6.5).

Thus has God taught us that through obedience to Christ and our love for him we may love ourselves. We turn now to his commands to love others in the same way that we love ourselves.

Notes

[1] The word *existential* has a bad name among many Protestant evangelicals because of it association with some secular philosophies and heretical theologies over the past century. However, it remains a perfectly good and accurate word for the reality of *experience*, or of a thing *existing*, as opposed to our intellectual ideas *about* the thing. Jesus and the gospel are *existential* facts, eternal "givens," not something deduced from something else. They are that by which all else is measured.

[2] The first law of thermodynamics states that matter is neither created nor destroyed; this is the law of conservation of energy. The second law of thermodynamics states that in the transformation from one state of matter to another (wood, for example,

being burned and transformed into heat, smoke and ash), the form, or structure, is reduced to a lower order. This is *entropy*, decay. It is both a scientific question and a theological one.

[3] Whether or not the Adam and Eve story is "true" in a literal sense is irrelevant. The truth of it lies in what God is showing us by means of the story about our human condition and our relationship to him.

[4] In Hebrew folklore, a heathen deity, supreme among evil spirits. Literally, "lord of flies."

[5] The test of the Christian is his acknowledgment of the deity of Jesus. Jesus himself poses the critical question to his disciples when he asks, " . . . who do you say that I am?" (Matthew 16.15), and Peter answers, "You are the Christ, the Son of the living God" (v. 16). To speak, as some do, of well-meaning non-believers as "better Christians" than some who acknowledge his deity is nonsense. It implies that well-doing is a substitute for belief. This has long been a popular heresy, but it won't hold up. To those "better Christians" who do not believe, Jesus' answer, as we saw, is devastating: "I never knew you; depart from me, you evildoers" (Matthew 7.23).

[6] Kenneth S. Wuest, *The New Testament, an Expanded Translation* (Grand Rapids, 1956).

[7] C. S. Lewis, *The Great Divorce* (New York, 1957), p. 69.

[8] The late Charles Williams put these thoughts in a statement that should be memorized by every lover: "The famous saying, 'God is love', it is generally assumed, means that God is like our immediate emotional indulgence, and not that our meaning of love ought to have something of the 'otherness' and terror of God" (*He Came Down from Heaven*, p. 15).

[9] *The Philokalia, the Complete Text*, Vol. 2, p. 43.

[10] *Ibid.*, p. 363.

C.
TO OBEY GOD IS
TO LOVE OTHERS

Chapter Eight

WE ARE SENT

Out of our concern for loving and obeying God flows love for our neighbors. Our neighbors are those nearest us, not necessarily physically next door. They are those for whom God has given us responsibility: spouse, children, employees, friends, business associates, as well as those needing our help whom God has placed in our path.

We have seen in the preceeding section how we are to love ourselves just as God loves us and how it is through obedience to his Son that we, fallen and errant, sick and despicable creatures though we are, are *able* to love ourselves. Now comes the command: "You shall love your *neighbor* as [in the same way, in the precise degree to which you love] yourself." It appears in all of the first three gospels. The original Hebrew that Jesus was quoting (Leviticus 19.18) is even more emphatic. It reads, "You shall love your neighbor *as if he were yourself!*" Strong stuff! When it comes to loving, we are to make not even the slightest distinction between ourselves and our neighbor!

In this and the next chapter we will examine closely what this implies. Now the going gets a little heavier, for two reasons: 1) some theological issues have at least to be noted; and 2) we are up against our modern culture, which is manifestly self-serving, negligent of neighbors, filled with self-admiration, and drifting determinedly away from God.

What is our *first* concern for our neighbor? The command appears in Mark 16.15. It comes after Jesus' resurrection, and he is addressing the eleven remaining apostles; it is among his last words to them: "Go into all the world and preach the gospel to the whole creation." The passage in Matthew is more dramatic and states the command even more urgently:

Now the eleven disciples went to Galilee, to the mountain
to which Jesus had directed them. And when they saw him
they worshiped him; but some doubted. [Who wouldn't?
This is something radically new on earth.] And Jesus came
and said to them, "All authority in heaven and on earth has
been given to me. Go therefore and make disciples of all
nations, baptizing them in the name of the Father and of
the Son and of the Holy Spirit, *teaching them to observe
all that I have commanded you*; and lo, I am with you
always, to the close of the age" (Matthew 28.16-20).

This is commonly called the "Great Commission," and it is
clearly meant for Jesus' followers throughout all earthly time.
Our major concern with respect to our neighbor is to tell him
the good news (gospel) of the saving grace of Jesus Christ, and
to present his commands. Someone will immediately protest:
no, our first concern is to feed and clothe him, bind up his
wounds (as in the parable of the Good Samaritan), give him
something to drink and see that he is cared for. True, Jesus
did command this. But he indicates that much more than the
physical act is implied: *he* is involved, we are acting on *his* behalf,
we are *his agents*, as we see in Matthew 10.40-42. Is the reci-
pient not to know this? It is all a "package," as we say, and Christ
is at the center. After all, the government, which knows nothing
of Christ, can give food, water and every sort of material good
in billion dollar packages with no Christ in them – and the spiritual
hunger and thirst will go on. While remembering the Good
Samaritan, we need also to remember the Samaritan woman
at the well, who came to fetch merely physical water and
departed with Christ's "living water" besides (John 4.7-26).

We are Plunged into a Jungle

Let us make no mistake. If we are, in love, to fulfill the Great
Commission it presupposes that we are in a state of obedience
to all the other commands we have discussed thus far; otherwise we are in no state to proclaim anything about Christ, for

we know him only at a distance, if at all.

But assuming we are ready, then what? We are immediately plunged into a jungle, and the snakes, serpents and vipers – all the forces of Satan – instantly mount their attack against us, and we are forced to behave as one must in a jungle and be wary and wise, clever and perceptive, and *absolutely sure of our way.*

As Jesus commanded, we are to "be wise as serpents and innocent as doves" (Matthew 10.16). "Wise" here implies prudence as to one's own safety. "Wary" would be more accurate. "Innocent" means that our methods are to be without guile, falsity or subterfuge.

This is not the place for a discussion of evangelical techniques. Rather, our purpose, as we stated in Chapter 1, is to find the way of wisdom, which is the way of love and obedience, and to do that we must learn something about the jungle where our adversaries prowl and seek to devour us together with our message (1 Peter 5.8).

The Apostles, loving their Lord, obeyed the command. Upon receiving the Holy Spirit at Pentecost,[1] they were galvanized into action, and received power. Peter and John healed, and preached in the Temple to the Jews. Philip went to Samaria and baptized and preached; Peter went to Lydda, then to Joppa, then to the household of Cornelius the Centurion at Caesarea when it was revealed to him that the gospel was to be preached also to the Gentiles, exactly as Jesus commanded. The Church was now active and operating, and had begun to carry out the Great Commission. All this is described in the book of Acts.

Then the persecutions began. Stephen was the first martyr (Acts 7.58). There were to be thousands more. Of the apostles, only John is believed to have died a natural death. But there was worse to come.

Worse? What could be worse for Jesus' disciples than torture and death? *Distortion and destruction of the gospel they had been commanded to preach and for which they were willing to die.*

Distorted it was, and almost destroyed. Presently the heresies began. Heresies are bad theology, distortions of the gospel, twistings of thought that change the clear and universal understanding of the gospel as held by the Apostles and by the disciples in the early Church; they include many dubious additions of speculative ideas that are no essential part of the gospel. They began early, and many are still with us. We cannot describe them all, for there were hundreds, but it is important that we be aware of the kind of thing that can becloud our understanding of the gospel, for when the old heresies appear in new dress they reassert themselves more strongly than before. Nor do those who say with a certain self-satisfaction, "We just stick to scripture!" have the answer, for virtually every heretic throughout history has claimed the authority of scripture. We will deal with this at least to some extent, for if we desire to love Jesus and obey him, nothing can be permitted to cloud our understanding of the gospel, especially as we preach it to others.

Distortions of the Gospel

One of the earliest distortions to inflict itself upon the Church was called Gnosticism, from the Greek word for "knowledge." As pagan Greeks were converted to Christianity, they brought with them into the Church pagan ideas derived from Greek mythology and philosophy. (In Chapter 11 we will consider some of the influences of pagan philosophy that wrought devastation in theology, especially in the West, and persist even today.) The early Gnosticism was introduced largely by intellectuals who found the gospel too simple and earthly and introduced Greek notions of the "ideal." These appeared under various names at different times but the thrust of them was: 1) Christians possess a special secret "knowledge" which sets them apart; and 2) matter is essentially evil and in opposition to the spirit, so that one must eventually destroy the other.[2] This was insupportable from the standpoint of the gospel, for God made matter and "it was very good" (Genesis 1.31). And Jesus Christ came *in the flesh* (matter); God did not disdain to participate in matter. Moreover, he came *for all*, not just for a few who had a "secret knowledge" of him.

All this may seem for us today fairly obvious, but it was a real threat then, for a "gnostic" faith would have been no Christian faith at all. Yet even today there are those who preach a Christianity of "ideals," an etherialized gospel.

A more serious distortion broke out around A.D. 318. There was a priest named Arius, educated in the theological school at Antioch,[3] who later moved to Alexandria in Egypt. The thought of the Antiochian school was very down-to-earth, but Arius carried it too far. He preached that the Son is a subordinate creature to the Father and therefore not truly God, a lesser deity perhaps, but not really divine. Such doctrine undercuts the foundation of the gospel. It would make the Wise Men (Matthew 2.11), Peter and the other Apostles (Mark 8.29; Matthew 14.33; 28.9,17) and all those in the New Testament and throughout history, including ourselves, who have worshiped Jesus, worshipers of a creature – idolaters! However, Arius' reasoning had a tremendous "logical" appeal, and for a time the dominant theology of the Church was Arian. This may have been due in part to Arius' personality – he was charming and learned, intelligent and persuasive; he would today be a highly successful TV preacher. The Church's response to Arius was the Council of Nicaea in A.D. 325 and the Nicene Creed, which affirms that Christ was "begotten, not made," "begotten of the Father before all worlds" and truly God.

We will mention only one other distortion that appeared in the early Church, out of many that could be mentioned. It is called Pelagianism. Pelagius was a learned and devout monk from Britain who went to Rome around A.D. 400 and was shocked at the laxity of spiritual life there. He perceived the cause of this to be too great dependence on Christ; the Church seemed to be saying: you can do nothing to save yourself, only Christ can save you, so it makes no difference how you behave as long as you remain in the Church and trust Christ. Pelagius began to preach essentially the reverse of this: you *can* save yourself without Christ; you have but to discipline yourself and do good and call on Christ for help when you think you need him.

Both extremes are wrong. The gospel is that indeed only Christ can save us, but he will not do it against our will. It is a matter of voluntary submission of our wills to his. However, these extremes still appear in many churches today.

There is only one way that distortions of the gospel can be effectively dealt with, and that is for the Church as a whole to meet in council, to pray, to discuss, and to seek as one body the direction of the Holy Spirit, and let the result become the "mind of the Church." It is notable that distortions (heresies) all tend to arise from individuals putting their own interpretations on scripture apart from the understanding of the Church as a whole, attracting what followers they can, then forming a new sect. Individualism is ever a deterrent to the gospel. This did not mean that a majority vote in council decided everything. Rather, the council did the best it could, then the results were *tested in practice,* seeking confirmation or rejection by the Holy Spirit (1 John 4.1). Division was inconceivable to the early Church, for the gospel of Christ is one. Unfortunately, the last general (ecumenical) council of the Church was Nicaea II, in A.D. 787. Christendom today cries out for another general council.

Warnings for Today

We tend today to think of ourselves as more "advanced," tolerant, and capable of reconciling issues than was the early Church, but we are not. We are more fragmented, and there is no unifying authority such as was supplied by the Church Councils and by the Emperors from Constantine starting in A.D. 323 on until the Great Schism between East and West in A.D. 1054. There are other deterrents as well to the straightforward gospel Christ commanded his followers to preach. The warnings in scripture apply even more urgently to us than they did to the early Church. In Hebrews we are warned: "Do not be led away by diverse and strange teachings . . ." (13.9). And by Saint Paul in his letters to Timothy: "Now the Spirit expressly says that in later times some will depart from the faith by giving heed to deceitful spirits and doctrines of demons, through the pretensions of liars . . . " (1 Timothy 4.1,2); and " . . . preach the word . . . convince, rebuke and exhort . . . the time is coming when people will not endure sound teaching, but having itching ears they will accumulate for themselves teachers to suit their own likings . . . " (2 Timothy 4.2,3).

We stated in Chapter 1 that in our "modern" Western society much that was crystal sharp for early Christians has become blurred. We have become superficial, and our worship sentimental. Our culture is self-centered and narcissistic. We mentioned "simpering, self-centered songs." The following are some lines selected more or less at random from the sheet music in a "Christian" bookstore: "I am loved, I am loved, I can risk loving you." "I got love, love in my heart; I got peace like a river." "Well, I don't understand this love I have inside. Would it be the same without the twinkle in your eye?" "How can I say thanks for the things you've done for me?" "I see dark clouds coming my way — I know they're going to rain on me." This is purportedly "gospel'" music. Its relationship to the gospel is obscure, to say the least. Someone will immediately say, "Well, *I* don't see anything wrong with it!" Of course not. It is so much a part of our culture that no one notices, and it rakes in millions of dollars. And it is utterly wrong. Note that in just those few lines the pronoun "I" is repeated ten times. The focus is entirely on self. Adoration of God, contrition, heartfelt thanks to God, humility, self-abnegation, the discipline of obedience, all the essential elements of the Christian Way of Life are missing. There is no virility in it, and not a shred of *agape*. In a climate of such maudlin sentimentality it is difficult to preach the gospel.

Another hindrance is our fascination with prophecy. We are often told we are in the "end times." There is so much of this flowing from the "electronic pulpit" that one can hardly mention anything about "church" without someone raising the question of "rapture."

"Rapture" is a popular term referring to the time when Christians will be caught up "to meet the Lord in the air . . . " as foretold by Saint Paul in 1 Thessalonians 4.17. It is also prophesied by Christ himself in Matthew 24 and Mark 13. The question is *when* it will happen in chronological time (Greek *chronos*), but Jesus said that even he did not know (Mark 13.32). And in Acts 1.7 he says, "It is not for you to know times or seasons which the Father has fixed by his own authority." Yet we have preachers today who presume to know!

At issue is the question whether the "rapture" will take place *before* the "great tribulation" prophesied in the 6th and 7th chapters of the book of Revelation or afterward. Speculations about this and other prophesies in scripture can go on endlessly. For our purpose in understanding obedience and love and finding the Way of Life, the following observations are perhaps worthwhile.

1. We are much too concerned with *chronos* (chronological time). We keep wanting to know where we stand with respect to God's timetable for the world, as if God were bound by a time track. The New Testament is more concerned with *kairos*, another Greek word for "time," often translated "the right time" or "the fullness of time." We should consider the possibility that events may not happen sequentially, but at differing "times" in different places. It is possible that *all* the years since Christ constitute the "end times." The Apostle Peter wrote, "The end of all things is at hand . . . " (1 Peter 4.7). And John, the "beloved disciple," wrote, " . . . it is the last hour; and as you have heard that antichrist is coming, so now many antichrists have come . . . " (1 John 2.18). There has probably not been a generation since Christ but has felt it was in the "end times" and that the "last hour" was at hand. At any given moment in history there seem to be antichrists scattered everywhere. It would appear that for the Russians and for the Chinese Christians the antichrist assuredly has come and the tribulation is upon them. The Jewish "holocaust" gets a great deal of publicity. Satan, however, has managed to suppress an equally widespread awareness of the millions upon millions of Christians slaughtered by the Communists. Satan has also managed to discount in the minds of most people the heinousness of the slaughter of well over 15 million unborn babies since the Supreme Court in 1973 permitted abortion on demand.

2. The notion of a "pre-trib rapture" has never existed in the doctrines of the historic Church. It began with the vision of a Scottish girl by the name of Margaret MacDonald in 1830, and then caught on with some groups promoting highly individualistic notions in the nineteenth century.[4] (The fact that so much "Christian" prophecy that was highly touted in the nineteenth century just didn't pan out seems to daunt our contemporary "prophets" not at all.) This novel doctrine is popular today because it supplies excitement and attracts money, as the essential Christian doctrines of repentance, humility, suffering and self-denial do not. It is especially tragic that it was preached by many churches in China before the revolution, so that Christians were not prepared for the tribulation when it came. For the Christian, the only viable attitude is obedience to the command of Jesus in Mark 13.35-37: *watch!* (We will have more to say about this in our Chapter 11.) Jesus gave many warnings about this. We are to hold ourselves constantly in readiness to meet him, as he tells us in the parable of the faithful and unfaithful stewards in Luke 12.35-47, and in his charge to the Church at Pergamum to "repent" (Revelation 2.16). To be ready is to have confessed and repented our sins, loved God and our neighbor, and to have obeyed Jesus' commands. Slippery sinners that we are, would we trouble ourselves to do all that if we knew the final hour? No, we'd amuse ourselves with earthly enjoyments up to the very last instant, and then it might be too late. It is never too early to begin to prepare.

Speculations about prophecy tend to be prideful and self-assertive, contributing nothing to our understanding of humility, obedience and love. A contemporary monk of the Russian Church, who died in Finland in 1958, has expressed it well: "A humble man is not curious about incomprehensible things, but a proud man wants to investigate the depth of God's dispensations."[5] And, "We are told well and clearly in Holy Scripture how to be saved, but our limited and inquisitive little minds are not satisfied with this and want to know something more about the future . . . "[6] Yet over and over again we get "fashions" in prophecy touted by individuals who then gather a following and create a new division in the body of Christ. Individualism, as we have said, is ever a handicap to the gospel.

3. Another novel doctrine, unknown to the historic Church and frequently tied to the notion of a "pre-trib rapture," is "Christian Zionism," which lends vigorous support to the militant secular state of Israel as a supposed fulfillment of prophecy. Millions upon millions of dollars have been poured into this secular State by many thousands of pious Christians in the belief that they were supporting God's plan of salvation. As justification for such support, militant Zionists and others have cleverly cited Old Testament promises that the Jewish people would be given the land of Palestine. But the historic position of the Church has been from the beginning that all the Old Testament prophecies and promises are fulfilled in Christ. Throughout his letters Saint Paul hammers at the theme that it is those who believe in the Lord Jesus Christ who are the true sons of Israel: " . . . if you are Christ's, then you are Abraham's offspring, heirs according to promise" (Galatians 3.29). Between Jew and Gentile there is no difference, but all are one in Christ — if they accept him. Saint Paul makes this clear in Ephesians 2.11-18. There is no return of Israel to the land, for that would now have to include all Christian Gentiles as well! *Christ's Church is the new Israel,* of which Jesus is King, and there is not nor ever can be any other Israel. The first historian of the Church, Eusebios of Caesarea, writing about the year A.D. 300, said, "The Jewish laws, as given to them by their fathers, have become null and void . . . the historic world mission of the people of Israel has been taken from them and has been given to the Christian Churches." The only possible attitude of Christians toward Jews is to love them as Jesus loved them and commanded us to love them, and *preach the gospel* to them that they too may be brought into the kingdom.[7]

The point for us is that these matters are peripheral to the gospel, which is that the Son of God became incarnate, suffered, died and rose again out of love for us, leaving specific commands which we are to obey if we are committed to loving him in return. Our attention must be on those commands.

Fulfilling the Great Commission

In Chapter 3 we discussed Jesus' command to Peter to follow him. We turn now to the clause that follows. Jesus was walking by the Sea of Galilee and saw Simon (Peter) and his brother, Andrew, fishing, and he commanded them, "Follow me, and I will make you fishers of men" (Matthew 4.19). Luke's version is slightly different. It has Jesus getting into Peter's boat and telling him to let down his nets after a night of catching nothing, and the catch is so great that Peter has to call his partners, James and John, to help haul it in. We discussed in Chapter 3 what this implies as to provision of our physical needs if we obey Jesus' commands. We see now that the physical catch is incidental; the important thing is to bring converts to Christ. Luke goes on to say, "And when they had brought their boats to land, they left everything and followed him" (Luke 5.10). Here, then, were the first four converts to Christianity: Peter and Andrew, James and John. The great enterprise of bringing men to God had begun. Luke implies that they did not even bother to dispose of the catch – all those rotting fish! But what are they, compared to bringing men to Christ?

Are we all then to become missionaries? In a certain sense, yes. If we love Jesus and obey him, our entire lives will be a witness to him. But before rushing off to the mission field we had better wait to be called – by the Church, which is Christ's body in which we live the new life today. Otherwise pride can enter, about which we will have more to say in a moment. Meanwhile there is a command that applies unequivocally to us all: "The harvest is plentiful, but the laborers are few; pray therefore the Lord of the harvest [the Father] to send our laborers into his harvest" (Luke 10.2). The word translated "send out," incidentally, implies something much stronger. It means "thrust out," "force out," as a matter of urgent necessity.

Several years ago I took the Laymen's Institute course of Campus Crusade for Christ, which gave instruction in how to witness. The last afternoon of the seminar we were sent out in pairs to witness in a residential neighborhood of Riverside, California.

Everyone was in a state of fear and trembling; we felt certain it was all an exercise in futility. I shall never forget that Saturday afternoon. At house after house we met indifference and some opposition, but at others when we said we wanted to speak about Jesus Christ and his love, we were welcomed with tears almost. The astounding lesson to me was that the harvest *is* plentiful; the neighborhood was a spiritual wasteland greater than the surrounding California desert, and *people were starving.* We are commanded to pray for laborers to work in those dry neighborhoods, *which are everywhere.*

After prayer, then what? Immediately following the passage about the harvest Jesus confers upon the twelve disciples authority to act in his name, and he commands them: "Heal the sick, raise the dead, cleanse lepers, cast out demons" (Matthew 10.8). A similiar passage occurs in Luke 9 and again in Luke 10, where the directive is to "seventy others" in addition to the twelve. The "seventy" were sent ahead, Luke says, into every town and place where Jesus was to come. Jesus did not instruct this group with respect to the dead, lepers, or demons, but they returned exclaiming to him, "Lord, even the demons are subject to us in your name" (Luke 10.17)! A fantastic new power had been released on earth by Jesus and authority to use it had been placed in the hands of his followers.

The Christian era is indeed something new on earth. Disciples throughout the ages have labored and loved, as Jesus commanded. Incredible developments have taken place in the way of healing and materiai benefits. In view of the authority Jesus conferred on his disciples, it would not be surprising if all illness had been swept from the earth and if all those who died prematurely had been raised from the dead, as Paul raised Eutychos (Acts 20:9-12). Why then has it not happened?

The question cannot be evaded. For "natural man," healing and material human benefits are all-important. Their imperfect fulfillment is even seen by some as a refutation of the Christian faith, and now we have government and a wealth of secular enterprises taking over to make up for the Christian "deficiency." There is an obsession with "human betterment," and in truth

God has permitted this. If we will but think about the question we will see the answer:

1. Perfect health is not necessarily an unmitigated blessing. It is often in pain and sorrow and suffering that we come to recognize our total dependence on God. Is it in perfect health that we love God most, and obey him? Or in suffering, when we most feel the need to have him?

2. Salvation is more important than health. The Great Commission is to *proclaim the gospel.* Healing is incidental.

3. Jesus said, " . . . what will it profit a man, if he gains the whole world [meaning *every* material benefit, including physical health] and forfeits his life [that is, eternal life]" (Matthew 16.26)? Even Jesus himself did not heal everyone; rather, his healing was, as we saw in Chapter 5, a demonstration of the gospel – *who he was.*

4. It is in praising and thanking him that we truly come near to God, as he desires us to. Yet of those healed today, how many praise him? The situation is no different now than it was in Jesus' time when he healed ten lepers and only a foreigner returned to praise and thank him (Luke 17.12-19).

5. Many devout persons have possessed healing power, but have been reluctant to use it, because it is a temptation to pride. The contemporary Russian monk whom we quoted earlier has written, "It is very dangerous to accomplish healing. If a righteous man turns prideful, God remembers only his sin. . . . Many a saint has been lost by coming to think, 'Oh, now I am a saint'. It is far safer to be a repentant sinner than a saint."[8] Humility and repentance before God are far more important than outward demonstrations of the power Christ bestowed on his followers. A collection of Christian writings tells of a young disciple who told his spiritual director that such and such a disciple "saw angels." His spiritual director answered, "This is not surprising, that he sees angels, but I would marvel at a person who saw his own sins."[9]

6. Truly to love our neighbor means above all to *let him be himself in God,* then *God will do for him and in him what is needed.* In the end it is not *we* who can do for him, or possess him, or manipulate him to any given end. He belongs to God,

and our standing ready, and waiting, and praying, and perhaps suffering on his behalf is in itself to love our neighbor.

That is something we need constantly to remember. We are a "*do*" generation. We are in love with techniques. We want everthing accomplished right now, and we are determined to get on with it – *on our own terms*. God's terms are a humble and a contrite heart, then *he* will get on with it – using us, if we are submitted to him in obedience and love.

Meanwhile, Jesus left specific commands for our personal relationships with one another. If we will obey them, then we will truly love him and our neighbor. We will examine these in the next chapter.

Notes

[1] Pentecost was a Jewish feast day fifty days after the Passover and the Resurrection. The disciples were gathered on that day, and dramatic events took place, signifying the beginning of the Church, as recounted in Acts 2.

[2] The early Church was on guard against those who tried to introduce a pagan "high-minded idealism" that disdained material things and denied their importance. Canon 51 of the "Canons of the Holy Apostles," a compilation of rules governing the early Church, reads: "If any bishop, presbyter or deacon . . . abstain from marriage, or flesh, or wine, not by way of religious restraint, but as abhoring them, forgetting that God made all things very good, and that he made man male and female, and blaspheming the work of creation, let him be corrected, or else be deposed, and cast out of the Church. In like manner a layman."

[3] Antioch, on the Orontes River near the Mediterranean on the northern coast of Syria, was one of the most prominent cities of the Roman and Byzantine Empires. From here Paul set out on his missionary journeys and Peter was for seven years leader of the Christian community. It was in Antioch that the disciples "were first called Christians" (Acts 11.26). Ancient Antioch is now in ruins, and the site is occupied by the small Turkish town of Antakiya.

[4] Excellent historical documentation of the idea of a "pre-trib rapture" is supplied in a book by Dave MacPherson, *The Incredible Cover-up* (Medford, Oregon, 1975).

[5] Father John, *Christ is in Our Midst* (Crestwood, N.Y., 1980), p. 134.

[6]*Ibid.*, p. 138.

[7] There are those who insist that the Jews are totally inaccessible. That is not true. They are certainly put off by the contempt in which Christians have historically held them, but there are groups at work converting the Jews. One of the most successful is a group who themselves are Jewish converts, called Jews for Jesus, located at 60 Haight St., San Francisco, CA 94102. A truly converted Jew is a beautiful creature to behold, for he has come into his heritage and is spiritually fulfilled. Yet these converts have been spat upon in the streets not only by their own fellow Jews but by Christians and contemptuously treated in some churches. They have learned, as many non-Jewish Christians have not, that it is costly to follow Christ.

[8]Father John, *Christ is in Our Midst,* p. 96.

[9]*Ibid.*, p. 5.

Chapter Nine

OUR LOVE FOR OTHERS

We have dealt thus far with the commands of Jesus relating directly to our loving and obeying God and to our loving ourselves. In the preceeding chapter we took up the command to love others, beginning with the Great Commission. We turn now to Jesus' specific commands that are to govern our relationships with *all persons*.

The Great Commission has to do with creating new Christians through words (preaching), one central action (baptizing), and teaching them to obey the commands of Jesus (Matthew 28.16-20). The commands we will now consider supply the formula for our daily lives with others. It is obvious from even a casual reading of the New Testament that, next to our personal relationship to him, God views right relationships to others as the most important thing in our lives. The relationships will be right to the extent that, in obedience to God, they are governed by love. God does not traffic in trivialties or place pleasant options before us. *He means his word to govern everything we do.*

The Way of Love

As we study obedience and love it is important that we know exactly what we are talking about. There are two ways to define "love." One is to *show* it in action; the other is to explain it in words. The gospels show us love in action in the person of Christ – what he does. A drama or a novel may also show love in action. But we are writing a discursive work. If our subject were some material matter, say horticulture, one could go look it up in an encyclopedia and find it fully defined, and then discuss it. But try finding "love" in an encyclopedia. It simply isn't there.

Yet it has been called "the greatest thing in the world!" So much for encyclopedias. For our purposes we have to be content with intuitive understandings, which are, after all, what wisdom mostly consists of. So before we proceed to the commands formulated by God to govern human relationships, let us amplify our understanding of love. *Then* appreciation will begin to flood in upon us of what Christ really meant when he said, "You shall love your neighbor *as* [in the same way, in that precise degree to which you love] yourself" (Matthew 22.39).

Someone will immediately ask, "Are you talking about *agape* or *eros*?" (See Chapter 2). The answer is, "both." Whatever categorical distinctions philosophers and theologians may try to make, the two cannot be completely separated. One always implies the other in some degree. *Eros* without *agape* tends toward sexual self-indulgence and lust. *Agape* without any touch of *eros* is likely to drift toward a sterile "idealism," a sort of "high-mindedness" indifferent to the fact that in Christ God came to us *in the flesh.*

So let us examine further the nature of love:

In Chapter 1 we spoke of the Way of Life and the Way of Death. *Love is the Way of Life.*

The loveless way is the way of death, murder, war and defeat. The way of victory is love.

Love is not one technique among many – it is everything, or nothing.

Love is the assertion of the New Covenant over the Law (techniques).

Love is Christ in us, the living truth.

Love is the present reality of the Holy Spirit filling us.

Love is not self-conscious; it loses itself in the good, for the sake of others.

Love is not possessive. It does not attempt to arrogate to itself the personhood of another.

Love is wisdom, and wisdom-in-action is courtesy and submission toward God and man.

Love is not indulgent of sentimental immaturity, but desires for the other the full stature of spiritually mature adulthood in Christ.

Love is never a vague or general beneficence; it is pulsatingly real, an engine of concern and action — most frequently, prayer — specifically directed toward individual persons.

Love is that which in the depth of our hearts we most earnestly desire; it is the satisfaction of a yearning implanted there by God when he created us. It is the fractious Adam in us that puts love aside and tries to accomplish on its own that which love wishes to accomplish in and for us. But we will not accept the humbling that this requires; we enjoy the rebellious contrarity of the Adam in us, and as a consequence we hate God (who is love) because he interferes with what we in our *self*-assertion have determined *we* will do.

Love is gladly obedient unto death for the sake of the good that is commanded of it.

Love is not contingent upon circumstances. However, when it is mocked or persecuted, it can and will hide itself as Jesus did (John 8.59). It will also retreat when asked to cater to the selfish desires of another or to a whim rather than a need. We are not to cast the pearls of love before swine (Matthew 7.6). Hidden, however, it is still there. It may suffer, and even be put to death, but it cannot be extinguished.

Love lives in obedience to God — the commands of Christ. Without that obedience it has no source, no roots; it dies for lack of nourishment.

Where do we find love? Not here, not there, nor at such and such a time (Luke 17.21). It is not a clock matter, nor a calendar matter, nor a matter of physical place. It is a "fullness" matter (see preceeding chapter), a condition within ourselves, an attitude of mind, heart and spirit. It is a *state of being* which we discover when we are *obedient to Christ's commands.*

It is in the fullness of the *moment of love* that we discover *who we are* and *who is our neighbor* and *experience the fullness of heaven* in our midst. All this happens in the *moment of obedience,* not in a time of thought, reflection, philosophical musings — or of disobedient action.

Until the day when we obey the commands of Jesus we

cannot love, or live, for he is the Lord of Love and giver of the Way of Life. Until we obey him, we are the walking dead – like the Scribes and Pharisees, whitewashed tombs (Matthew 23.27). It is Jesus, and he alone, who resurrects us as he did Lazarus and others; or, rather, it is by participation in *his* resurrection through obedience to his commands (as were Lazarus and Jairus' daughter and the son of the widow of Nain) that we receive life. Otherwise, we do not love God and he is not our God, for " . . . he is not God of the dead, but of the living" (Luke 20.38).

Admittedly, there is natural love. For in love God made us, and he implanted in the child a natural instinct to love and obey its parents. But then come rebellion and disobedience and the falling away of love for parents and for God. Also, there are those who may obey Jesus more or less accidentally. They absorb it from their surroundings. We are, after all, or were, a Christian culture. The Christian spirit still to a degree pervades our environment. We live on the accumulated grace poured out to our forefathers (and mothers), the residue of their piety and obedience. Remnants from the devotion of the Middle Ages are still with us. But this is diminishing and passing away, and we see the evidence in rising crime, terrorism, divorce, abortions, moral decline and general disrespect for life and for the commands of Jesus. If we look only to secular reasons for this, we find ourselves in a materialistic labyrinth leading to such presumed "rescuers" as Freud and Marx. But this is only Satan torturing us and leading us on in confusion and disarray far from the love of Christ. The true reason lies in the vanishing reservoir of love and obedience to God in the world around us. The well is going dry, and the well of loneliness and hate and disregard for God, ourselves and others is filling. In our casual pleasures and superficial living we are spiralling downward into the abyss of a stupid life and a stupid death. But God desires us to be, with him, triumphant!

Do we begin now to understand why out of his love for us Jesus *commands* us to love God, ourselves and our neighbor?

The Grand Co-inherence

The teachers of the early Church understood this well. They lived in the midst of a pagan world, and they were aware that the Son of God/Son of Man had come to establish a new way of life – *the* Way of Life without which there was for men *no life* but only a living death. Jesus declared to his followers that their lives were to be found in a tight-knit co-inherence involving God, their neighbors, and their own self-worth. The early teachers took this up and coined several classic aphorisms: Clement of Alexandria (A.D. 155-215) wrote, "He demands of us our lives for the sake of each other."[1] And Antony the Great of Egypt (A.D. 251-356) proclaimed, "Your life and your death are with your neighbor."[2]

It is less well understood today. We live in a new era of paganism. It has been called the "post-Christian" era, and indeed it is, but the tragedy is that no longer does the Christian Way of Life implicitly stand in judgment over the pagan, for Christians have invited the pagan to invade their way of life to the extent that the pagan rot is now well established in their midst. Our churches have become extremely tolerant of self-love, "buying" the world's "act." We settle for parodies of love instead of insisting on the real thing. Of how many Christians can it be said today, as the pagans said of the early Christians, "See how they love one another!"? But Jesus said they were to be the "salt of the earth" and that if they lost that character they were fit for nothing but to be thrown out and trodden underfoot (Matthew 5.13). It is happening now. Disobedient, we lose God's support and protection and fall victim to the paganism with which we compromise. We should instead be heeding the words of Peter on the Day of Pentecost, "Save yourself from this crooked generation" (Acts 2.40). To find love, and to be loved, and to love one another, we must devote ourselves to obedience to Jesus' commands. Yet we spend most of our time evading or compromising those commands, saying "No!" or "Maybe," or "I'll see" to Christ. We are lukewarm to God.

One way in which we evade and compromise is to let "love thy neighbor" mean for us a sort of vague goodwill, especially

toward far-off peoples about whom we know little. We are today remarkably reticent about sending missionaries to those people to preach the Gospel and baptize them as Jesus commanded
in the Great Commission. We are content instead to have our
Congress vote billions in all sorts of loans and aid to furnish
material benefits, regardless of the consequences to them and
to us. In our time, as in that of the gloomy Preacher in Ecclesiastes, " . . . money answers everything" (Ecclesiastes
10.19).[3]

So then even today many ask, like the lawyer in Luke 10.29,
"And who is my neighbor?" Jesus' answer was the story of the
Good Samaritan, and the implications for us today are perfectly
plain: our neighbor is the person God has placed in our immediate path and for whose well-being he has given us responsibility. It begins with the persons nearest and most needing us: wife
or husband, brother and sister, parents, the person next door
or at the next desk. It is above all those for whom we of our
own will assumed responsibility: our spouses and our children.

To what extent do we identify with these nearest us? Do
we take upon ourselves their sorrows, hurts, disappointments
exactly as if they were our own? We are so commanded. When
a son or daughter is trying to work through a difficult decision
– to date someone or not, plans for college, deciding on a right
action – are we *there*, ready to bring to bear what wisdom we
have acquired? Do we *show* that we are available? Do we *feel*
the anguish of the deciding process? Do we help them work
it through, *in love*? Or do we say, "You'll have to learn to decide
for yourself!"? But that is a brush-off, a cop-out. It is not love.
And how about husband or wife? Does one truly share to the
very depths the other's griefs, privations, burdens, afflictions and
concerns? Too commonly our attitude is, "Aw, c'mon, forget
it." In other words, "Don't bother me, *I* don't want to suffer."
Thus do we leave our neighbor to suffer alone, and nail Christ
again to the cross.

To entertain a vague goodwill toward others, far-off or even
nearby, is not at all to love our neighbor. If we will but set to
work to crucify or own petty selves and begin truly to identify

with those nearest us, taking on a Christlike role of humble service to them, we have a lifetime's task ahead of us, to be worked
at day by day in every situation, in every relationship with others,
and *nothing else is our business.* Colliander suggests the attitude
and technique required: " . . . the lower the position of service
you have, the freer you are. . . . Hold back your remarks . . .
Contradict nobody and do not get into arguments; let the other
person always be right. Never set your own will above that of
your neighbor. This teaches you the difficult art of submission,
and along with it, humility. *Humility is indispensable* [our
emphasis]."[4]

We see, then, that every situation in our lives, every relationship, every experience, every encounter, every condition,
every action is to be an occasion for us to practice humility, self-
denial and love – and in love, prayer. Never are we to let it be
occasion to parade our conceits, prejudices, animosities, touch-
iness, irrascibility, cleverness or any other indulgence of self-
love. But, having done *in love* all that is required of us, then
stand (Ephesians 6.13), knowing we can safely entrust the consequences to God.

We return now to C. S. Lewis' Mark and Jane Studdock
in Chapter 2. Mark, you will recall, had gone off to satisfy his
ambitions as part of an "in group" that was going to remake the
world. Jane had selfish ambitions of her own. Neither was submitted to the other. Mr. Fisher-King told her, " . . . you do not
fail in obedience through lack of love, but you have lost love
because you never attempted obedience." Obedience to what,
or whom? Obedience to her commitment to the marriage relationship and to her husband to whom she was trothed (pledged,
given in *truth*) by her own free action. Today it is the fashion
to think that marriage is just two individuals thrown together
for mutual self-satisfaction. It won't work, for neither love nor
truth are in it. The *self* must be eliminated, or there can be no
love. Mark's project blew up, and he returned chastened. Jane
repented her self-seeking independence and became obedient
to the requirements of the marriage relationship – a wife in *truth*
(troth). *Then,* the story implies, love returned.[5]

Elimination from the marriage service of the woman's promise to "obey this man" has been hailed as signalling women's liberation from male tyranny. It is something less than that. As usual, we have thrown out traditions hallowed by experience, negligent of what we are discarding; we see only the surface meaning of the words and ignore the deeper significance. For one is never so free as when fulfilling one's proper role in life. The man's role is to love and protect his woman, *bestowing honor upon her as the weaker sex* (1 Peter 3.7). *Her obedience consists in accepting and responding to his leadership, his love, honor and protection of her.* His is the active, masculine principle in operation. There are some situations in life that a woman simply cannot deal without degrading herself as a woman. The man with his push and shove and natural aggressiveness is meant to deal with them and defend her. So when a husband is properly doing his job, her obedience is a natural thing, quite in order, and not in the least demeaning. On the other hand, the woman is never more insecure than when she feels her husband is *not* protecting her, is not concerned with her as a person but only as a playmate or a domestic convenience.

But what do we get today? He sends her out into the job market to compete with men and take a battering from the world! (This is not to say wives should never work outside the home; they can, and often must – by mutual consent and understanding. However, the sex roles remain basically unchanged.) Worse, he may turn his natural aggressiveness *against her!* Should we be surprised at the divorce rate? It is in obedience to God's order of things that love grows, and in love that we seek increasingly to obey.

To love our neighbor in the same way, to exactly the same degree, that we love ourselves is a sacrifice, an offering made holy by obedience to the real needs of our neighbor, and thus to God. It is a kind of crucifixion in which we *die to self.* Jesus could not have been more emphatic: he commands that we love one another "*as I have loved you*" (John 13.34, 15.12). Again, the little word "as," meaning *in the same way, to the precise degree.* It is in the manner and depth of our loving our neighbor that we become like Jesus, fully identified with him, especially in his crucifixion.

This is strong stuff. Can we do it? Yes, with divine help. Is it worth it? What do we get in return? Here's what: " . . . if we love one another, God abides in us and his love is perfected in us" (1 John 4.12). To get the full import of that, consider it in the Phillips translation: " . . . if we love one another God does actually live within us, and his love grows in us toward perfection." *God and all his love in us!* Can anyone really want something more or better than *that?*

We Strip Ourselves of Power

Someone will now say, "Fine! So what's the program? What do we *do?*" This is the masculine principle at work with a vengeance. It is the dominant principle in our society. But Jesus' positive program we have already discussed in the preceding chapter: we are to preach the Gospel, baptize, heal, etc. For the rest of our relationships with others there is in the commands of Jesus a certain emphasis on what we are *not* to do. Always in our relationship to God, regardless of how "masculine" we may be, ours is a passive role. It is *God* who acts through us; we put our fate in his hands and let him use us. Let us consider his commands, however contrary they may be to our fallen natural impulses.

Jesus said, "Do not resist one who is evil. But if any one strikes you on the right cheek, turn to him the other also . . . " (Matthew 5.39). Vengeance is out. This is indeed a new thing, distinctive of the new Way of Life and love. The old was an "eye for eye, tooth for tooth," etc. (Exodus 21.24). God will handle the revenging (Romans 12.19).

Instead of defending ourselves, we are to come to terms with our accuser (Matthew 5.25). We are not to expect justice in a secular court. We are to get rid of our own sin before we concern ourselves with someone else's. " . . . first take the log [beam, plank, railroad tie, large obstruction] out of your own eye, and then you will see clearly to take out the speck that is in your brother's eye" (Luke 6.42). We are not to condemn or judge anyone else, or we invite God's judgment upon ourselves (Luke 6.37). Antony the Great of Egypt (A.D. 251-356) comments: " . . . not to judge anyone or to say that he is wicked and has sinned, is to render the soul inviolate. One should search out one's own faults and scrutinize one's own way of life, to see whether it conforms to God. What concern is it of ours if another man is wicked?"[6] Sin is like tar; you can't remove it from the other fellow without getting some on yourself. This emphatically does not mean, however, that society should not remove from its midst criminals that imperil the lives and property of others. It can and must, in firmness and charity. The commands apply to our *personal* attitudes toward others. We are not to usurp God's power of judgment.

We are to humble ourselves, serving others. " . . . whoever would be great among you must be your servant . . . whoever would be first . . . must be your slave . . . " In this we imitate Christ (Matthew 20.26-28). And Jesus does more than say this, he *shows* it by washing his disciples' feet (in Jesus' time, a task assigned to the lowest servant in a household), telling them to do the same to one another (John 13.14).

Always, we are to do more than is required of us. " . . . if any one would sue you and take your coat, let him have your cloak as well . . . " (Matthew 5.40). "Coat" means a short jacket or tunic. "Cloak" is the outer garment (top coat). And " . . . if any one forces you to go one mile, go with him two miles" (Matthew 5.41). The Roman authorities, under their law, could force subject peoples to perform certain tasks, within limits, such as carrying a soldier's pack one mile. The Christian was to do, even for the hated Roman, more than the law required – out of love.

Then there is the command: " . . . as you wish that men would do to you, do so to them" (Luke 6.31). This is the familiar Golden Rule. It has been cited as the "core" of the Christian faith. It is no such thing. It is on the face of it a formula of calculated reciprocity – you scratch my back, then I'll scratch yours. As such, it is found in many pagan beliefs. For the Christian it has to be understood in the context of far more radical commands such as, "Love your enemies and pray for those who persecute you" (Matthew 5.44). Jesus says we are to do this " . . . so that you may be sons of [resembling, like unto] your Father . . . " (Matthew 5.45). In other words, we are not to calculate what we will get in return, but love, an inexhaustible resource because it flows from the infinite God, is to pour from us with fine impartiality. This is again strong doctrine, but for our good. One of the great early teachers explains: "Why did he command this? To free you from hatred, irritation, anger and rancor, and to make you worthy of the supreme gift of perfect love."[7] Though he condemned the hypocrisy of the Pharisees, Jesus on the cross said, "Father, forgive them; for they know not what they do" (Luke 23.34). And Stephen, the first martyr, cried out as he was stoned, "Lord, do not hold this sin against them" (Acts 7.60). Christ and Stephen are to be our models. At this point someone is sure to say, "All right, so much for the heroics. I am not a Stephen and certainly not Christ on the cross. I have no expectation of being a martyr or a saint. So what has this to do with me?"

The answer is that you have no choice, if you are to be a Christian. It is no disrespect to say that there is a sense in which Stephen had it easy. He had his time of glory. He made his speech before the council, setting forth the entire doctrine of salvation and clearly obeying his Lord's command to preach the Gospel, and he did it under the hardest of circumstances, knowing it could cost him his life. Then he was taken out and stoned, and he died, and it was all over. You and I have to die every day and sometimes a hundred times a day, and each death is in a sense no less than Stephen's. How merciful if it were finished once for all! But we fall back into old ruts and have to die all over again. It is our dear, sweet pride and monstrous egos (so petty in the sight of God) that must be crucified. Lucky are they who have spouses or close friends to help them do it. Most of us have to do it to ourselves beneath the onslaught of conscience – God's judgment. And were it not for the prayers of the crucified Christ, helped by the example of many Stephens, we could not do it at all.

What is our daily crucifixion? Perhaps you have not met it yet.

Sit down and think about your days. Your wife says something, and you give her a sharp and testy answer. It's time for you to die, time to kill the selfish pride that prompted the answer, ask God's forgiveness and hers, and ask God's grace to change your ways. It may not be a sharp answer but a secret sin, or an attitude of heart we know God hates in us. There is no need here to spell it all out. We can see it in ourselves. The point is that to kill these things is for us precisely what crucifixion means. Not just charity but heroism and martyrdom begin at home.

We Obey in Chastity and Courtesy

Home and family are also the scene of much else in the Christian life. The family is the supreme school of love and obedience to God. It is his Church in microcosm. There is a head: the husband-father, who stands in the role of Jesus Christ, obedient to God the Father, as was Jesus. There is his spouse, whose role is acceptance and obedience to the head, who conveys and expresses the love and authority of God, just as the members of the Church are obedient and accepting of the authority of Christ, who is head of the Church. And there are the children, who in the context of the family learn obedience and love and all the disciplines of being a Christian.

If someone immediately shouts, "It is *not* like that!" one can only answer that to the extent that it is not, to that extent are we sinful and fallen from obedience, for that is exactly how God meant it to be. It is in the holy love and obedience to God of the family that God's glory is manifest. In the proper family every human good is to be found, and nowhere is the anguish and wretchedness of sinful humankind more intensely manifest than in an unloving and disobedient family.

The family, in addition to the Church, is the arena of our sanctification – the deification we mentioned earlier, and the demonstration of every human virtue.

So intense is life in the family that every flaw and foible in every member is sooner or later found out, and here it may be corrected in love without waiting to be subdued in the harsh competition of life outside the home or in the brutal confines of a prison.

In the home, love is to be practiced, both *agape* and *eros,* according to the definitions set forth in Chapter 2 and earlier in this chapter. The family is *par excellence* the laboratory of the Way of Life and Love. No wonder it is being so viciously attacked today by Satan. But we need not give in, for God sets forth exactly the attitude and approach we are to take to defend our marriages against the evil one.

We begin with the man, for he is the one designated by God to be head of the family (Ephesians 5.23).

The command to him is chastity (to her as well, but it is he who sets the tone, and hers is an even more exacting role, as we will presently see). Chastity is an even less popular subject today than obedience, and understood scarcely at all. Most people think of it as meaning total abstention from sexual relations. That is not at all what it means. What it means is exercise of the sexual function *only in the context of obedience to God,* which means in the fidelity of marriage, and the term applies as much to thoughts as to deeds. Jesus' command is explicit: "You have heard that it was said, 'You shall not commit adultery' [7th commandment, Exodus 20.14]. But I say to you that every one who looks at a woman lustfully has already committed adultery with her in his heart" (Matthew 5.27,28). Note that Jesus says *a woman*; a man is not to *lust* even after his own wife!

What are males to do, then, when lustful desires assault them? The great teachers of the early Church, who were assuredly male, and tempted, found the answer in a passage of scripture that is abhorent to the modern liberal mind because it fails to see the symbolic meaning its writer undoubtedly intended. The passage is the famous one in Psalm 137 about the "Babylonian babies." Verses 8 and 9 are rendered in *The Jerusalem Bible* as follows:

> Destructive daughter of Babel,
> a blessing on the man who treats you
> as you have treated us,
> a blessing on him who takes and dashes
> your babies against the rock![8]

Babel (Babylon) is the evil seductress in our imagination, and
the "babies" the temptations to which she gives birth. John Cas-
sian (A.D. 360-435) writes: "While the children of Babylon —
by which I mean our wicked thoughts — are still young, we should
dash them to the ground and crush them against the rock, which
is Christ . . . "[9]

C. S. Lewis states it best for moderns: "Against all such pretty
infants [our temptations to lust] the advice of the Psalm is best.
Knock the little bastards' brains out."[10]

Jesus extends the definition of adultery even to remarriage
after divorce. He declares: "Every one who divorces his wife and
marries another commits adultery, and he who marries a woman
divorced from her husband commits adultery" (Luke 16.18).

Is there no way out? On the face of it, no. The law of the
way of love and obedience, the Way of Life, is either celibacy
or unmitigated monogamy. There is no remarriage except after
separation by death. If this seems intolerably harsh, we need
to remember that the new life in Christ is not easy, nor it is sus-
tainable by earthly strength; it requires the grace of Christ and
the comfort (empowerment) of the Holy Spirit, who is for that
reason called the "Comforter" or "Strengthener," whom the
Father sends at Jesus' bidding (John 14.16). Let us remember,
however, that when we take our marriage vows before God and
the seal of his blessing comes upon our marriage, Jesus Christ
is the guarantor of our marriage, and with God "all things are
possible" (Mark 10.27). If, then, we call upon him to rescue
the marriage he has guaranteed, will he not answer? Provided,
of course, we persist, as we read in Chapter 4.

We are, however, human and fallible. None knows this better
than God, and he accepts repentance. In the West the Church
has handled this in one of two ways, either accepting the mistake and permitting remarriage; or by legalistic casuistry void-
ing the original "marriage," saying it never in fact existed. Orthodoxy takes a different attitude. It permits remarriage (but does
not encourage it), provided there is genuine repentance, for
St. Paul said, " . . . it is well for them to remain single . . .
[but] it is better to marry than to be aflame with passion"

(1 Corinthians 7.8,9). However, the *service of remarriage has a penitential character,* thus saying in effect, "Through his Church you are in your repentance forgiven by God and your marriage is blessed, but rely now all the more on his strength and mercy."

Adultery breaks the grand co-inherence of life that we spoke of earlier. It tears the web of love. It is gross disobedience to God.

We turn now to the woman's role. It is best explained in terms of the two great female prototyes in the Bible, Eve of the Old Testament and Mary of the New. We cannot here even begin to exhaust the truths displayed in the story of Adam and Eve, nor in the life of the historical Mary. We can see enough, however, to get some valuable insights into relations between the sexes today.

Eve was seduced. The serpent was, apparently, a very attractive creature. It was not until *afterward* that God cursed the serpent and ordained, " . . . upon your belly you shall go, and dust you shall eat . . . " (Genesis 3.14). Satan, who took the form of the serpent, can also be attractive. St. Paul says he can come as an "angel of light" (2 Corinthians 11.14). Eve said, "The serpent beguiled me, and I ate" (Genesis 3.13). Ate what? Not an apple, but of the *knowledge* of good and evil (Genesis 2.17). She introduced a knowledge humankind was never meant to have – knowledge of evil through disobedience. And as disobedience occurred, love was lost, for love is not compatible with disobedience.

Eve did what she was not meant to do. She took the initiative. It was not her business to make palaver with the serpent. She should have called Adam to deal with him, for he was meant by God to protect her. But she took the initiative in being disobedient. Even so, not all was lost, except that *Adam went along* with her disobedience and himself partook of the knowledge of evil! Worse, *he blamed her!* Still worse, *he blamed God!* He said to God, "The woman whom *thou gavest* to be with me, she gave me fruit of the tree, and I ate" (Genesis 3.12). Now if only he had said to God, "She sinned, and so did I. Punish me as you will, but forgive her, for mine is the greater sin. It was my job to protect her, but now that she has been disobedient

I intercede for her." For Adam was meant to be the high priest of all creation, including priest to his wife Eve. After all, God's original command about the "tree" was to Adam (Genesis 2.17); it was only afterward that God created Eve (Genesis 2.21). This could have been the beginning of selfless love, *agape,* but Adam declined even to intercede for the wife whom God had given him! He failed to be the priest, the man God meant him to be. It remained for Jesus Christ to take the punishment, to make the intercession, to be the "high priest," the man God meant Adam to be – to be in truth the New Adam.

The story diagrams exactly the situation we are in today. Women are angry at being betrayed, and rightly so. Many desire to "punish" men by taking on both masculine and feminine roles, saying, "I can be the man I always wanted my husband to be." Eve was first beguiled by the serpent, then sold out by her husband and is now deluded that she can be a man. It won't work. It will ruin her. She cannot be the man. It was a prescient insight from God that showed Moses (the author of Genesis) how women was created *from man* (Genesis 2.22), for today we know that in every cell of a man's body there are *both* the X (female) and Y (male) chromosomes, whereas a woman has not a Y chromosome in her body but instead *two* X chromosomes in every cell! God appears to have chosen to expand upon certain traits in man *through the woman,* to make her an enhanced, magnified part of the man. There are deep mysteries and implications here that remain to be fathomed.

The Submission of Mary

Mary is the opposite of Eve. Through her, love and obedience enter. The disobedience of Adam and Eve is rectified. Not that she was naive, for when the angel Gabriel appeared at the annunciation she asked, "How can this be, since I have no husband" (Luke 1.34)? But her final answer was, "Behold I am the handmaid of the Lord; let it be to me according to your word" (Luke 1.38).

The significance of this for us is eloquently expressed by the eminent Orthodox teacher Alexander Schmemann: " . . . in her love and obedience, in her faith and humility, she accepted to be what from all eternity all creation was meant and created to be: the temple of the Holy Spirit, the *humanity* of God. She accepted to give her body and blood – that is, her whole life – to be the body and blood of the Son of God, to be *mother* in the fullest and deepest sense . . . giving her life to the Other and fulfilling her life in Him. She accepted the only true nature of each creature and all creation: to place the meaning and, therefore, the fulfillment of her life in God."[11]

Mary's obedience represents far more than chastity. She is the "new Eve," reversing the disobedient curiosity of the old. As the old Eve introduced evil and transmitted it to her husband, so now Mary introduces single-minded goodness and becomes the God-bearing mother, the prototype of all obedient love for both men and women. Because of her obedience in bearing the Savior, men can now be what they were meant to be, priests of creation. Schmemann sums it up: "She stands for all of us, because only when we accept, respond in love and obedience – only when we accept the essential womanhood of creation – do we become ourselves true men and women; only then can we indeed *transcend* our limitations as 'males' or 'females.' For man can be truly man – that is, the king of creation, the priest and minister of God's creativity and initiative – only when he does not posit himself as 'owner' of creation and submits himself – in obedience and love – to its nature as the bride of God, in *response* and *acceptance*."[12]

This was the intuitive understanding of the early Church. It is a pity so much of it has been lost. In Protestant teaching the significance of Mary is largely ignored. This is a great loss, for Mary is in truth mother to all those who have been "born again." She is indeed the model of all motherhood as God meant motherhood to be, and the intimacy of her "motherhood of God" (in Greek, she is *Theotokos,* the God-bearer) reflects the closeness all men are thenceforth intended to have with God through his son. Roman Catholicism stresses Mary's virginity, which in itself means little, and even posits her "immaculate conception,"[13] a doctrine that is philosophically derived and quite

unscriptural. The stress of the early Church and of Eastern Orthodoxy today is on Mary's love, obedience and motherhood, from
which we have much to learn.

Love is Nobody's Patsy

For all our speaking of obedience and submission it might
seem that love is a pushover. Quite the opposite. Love is mature,
virile and discerning. In the face of opposition it may retreat for
a time, but it never gives up.

Love is circumspect. Jesus commands: "Take heed that no
one leads you astray" (Mark 13.5). He says, "Beware of false
prophets . . . " (Matthew 7.15) and "Beware of men . . . " (Matthew 10.17). This last refers to the opposition we are going to
meet when we practice our Christian faith in obedience to Jesus'
commands. For he says, " . . . they [men] will deliver you up
to councils, and flog you in their synagogues . . . " Obedience
in love will be persecuted. Worse, "Brother will deliver up brother
to death, and the father his child, and children will rise against
parents and have them put to death; and you will be hated by
all for my name's sake" (Matthew 10.21,22).

This has already happened in our time in the Marxist nations whose tribulation, as we said, has arrived. It is beginning
here. The State is already undertaking the interpretation of the
gospel.[14] The first amendment guarantees "free exercise" of
religion, but the bounds of that exercise are being increasingly
restricted by federal edict and the secular courts. Slice by slice
(the "salami" method) the areas in which Christians may apply
their convictions are being cut back. We are on the verge of
having Christian opposition to abortion and homosexuality, for
example, declared "contrary to public policy," in which case
churches could lose their tax-exempt status.

Yet in all this, even when our obedience to the commands
of God is thwarted, we are to trust God. Jesus said, "When they
deliver you up, do not be anxious how you are to speak or what
you are to say; for what you are to say will be given to you in
that hour; for it is not you who speak, but the spirit of your Father
speaking through you" (Matthew 10.19,20).

Thus again after 1,661 years (from Constantine, the first Christian emperor) must Christians practice obedience and love in the midst of a hostile, pagan world.

We turn now to consider love and obedience in and toward that body which is our home in Christ – his Church.

Notes

[1] Quoted by Charles Williams in *The Descent of the Dove* (New York, 1956), p. 46.

[2] *Ibid.*

[3] Many, if not most, costly political "do good" schemes have devastating effects that are just the opposite of what was intended. A brilliant factual analysis of this is set forth in the books of Thomas Sowell, a Senior Fellow at the Hoover Institution, and himself a black. See especially his *The Economics and Politics of Race* (New York, 1983).

[4] Colliander, *The Way*, p. 26.

[5] At least one contemporary radical movement seems to have thrown out any notion of the importance of love. They write: "We must destroy love . . . Love promotes vulnerability, dependence, possessiveness, susceptibility to pain, and prevents the full development of women's human potential by directing all her energies outward in the interest of others." *Women's Liberation: Notes from the Second Year, Major Writings of the Radical Feminists* (New York, 1970).

[6] *The Philokalia, the Complete Text*, Vol. 1, p. 342.

[7] Maximos the Confessor (A.D. 580-662), *ibid.*, Vol. 2, p. 59.

[8] *The Jerusalem Bible* (New York, 1966).

[9] *The Philokalia, the Complete Text*, Vol. 1, p. 77.

[10] C. S. Lewis, *Reflections on the Psalms* (London, 1958), p. 136.

[11] Alexander Schmemann, *For the Life of the World: Sacraments and Orthodoxy* (Crestwood, N.Y., 1973), p. 83.

[12] *Ibid.*, p. 85.

[13] A dogma of the Roman Church declared by the Pope in 1854 to be a required belief. It asserts that by God's special dispensation Mary was from the moment of her conception free from original sin. It has nothing to do with her virginity, which is a universally held Christian belief. The dogma has no support in scripture and tends to diminish her human status. There are those who argue that the Bible does not say, "a *virgin* shall conceive," but only "a young woman," citing the Hebrew word *almah* in Isaiah 7.14. But the Greek word in the New Testament is unequivocal; *parthenos* means *virgin*.

[14] As we write, a court case in California illustrates how the State is taking over interpretation of the gospel. Parents of a 24-year-old seminary student who committed suicide sued a church and the clergy who counselled him, alleging malpractice, negligence and outrageous conduct. The trial court found no substance to the allegations and threw out the case. The parents appealed. The appelate court reversed the trial court and introduced a new doctrine of "intentional infliction of emotional distress," saying the church was teaching that "suicide is an acceptable and even desirable alternative to living" – a grave distortion of what the church actually taught. The prospect of the secular courts defining the meaning of Christian doctrines is spine-chilling, holding as it does

the potential for shutting down all Christian teaching. The case is: *Nally v. Grace Community Church of the Valley*, 2 Civ. No. 67200 (Cal. Ct. App., 2d dist. June 28, 1984) (reversing summary judgment).

D.
TO OBEY GOD IS
TO LOVE HIS CHURCH

Chapter Ten

THE CHURCH BELONGS TO CHRIST

That place of the spirit in which we love Jesus, and obey him in love, is called the Church. It is his house. He invites us to live in it and to make it our home. We behave in it as we would in the home of our richest and most cherished friend to whom we owe more than we can ever repay, in fact everything. It is a beautiful place to live.

To say that, however, is not really to define "Church," for it cannot be defined. *Church is the experience of the kingdom,* and it eludes ordinary definitions. God does not permit them. The Church is his, and he will *show* us what it means by the experience of those who love, obey and serve him. That experience is shown us in scripture and by the testimony of the host of witnesses who have followed Christ.

Jesus plainly meant to establish his followers in one body where he would be with them, and which would carry forward the work he began. Thus if we are to be counted among his followers, we must love and serve his Church. The Greek word translated "Church" is *ekklesia,* meaning *that which is called out.* His followers, in other words, were "called out" from the world to be something different, set apart to be "the salt of the earth" (Matthew 5.13). In the latter part of this chapter we will examine more closely what this implies, and what we say there will rest on everything we have said in this book up to that point.

We must first, however, consider two "sacraments" (in Orthodox tradition, "mysteries") established by Christ and entrusted by him to the Church as the body by, through and in which they are performed, and without which they do not exist. They are baptism and the Eucharist. We may also say that without these sacraments the Church itself would not exist, for the Church is not just a gathering of Christians, a group of "members," a "meeting," a Bible study group, or a kind of "club." It is *the point of mediation between God and man.* It is *Christ in our midst* here and now; he is the mediator, and the sacraments are his instruments.

Baptism

"Sacrament" derives from the Latin *sacer* meaning "holy." But that does not tell us very much. We need to know what actually *happens* in a sacrament. In Chapter 3 we discussed Jesus' command, "Follow me," and we said that he so commands us because he loves us, and love desires to be closely identified with the beloved. Let us make no mistake; this is not just metaphorical talk; Jesus' love for us is the real thing, more real than any love that ever existed between human beings on earth; and we are to love him the same way in return. Then, having followed him, where do we arrive? In the kingdom of God (heaven), as we saw in Chapter 3. In other words, a *journey* is involved, a *pilgrimage.* We are going *from* somewhere *to* somewhere This is what "sacrament" in its deepest sense means.

This is a *spiritual* journey, but none the less *real* for being spiritual. There is nothing about Jesus or his Church or the sacraments that is "merely symbolic." That is, they are not just a "sign" but a reality of which the outward manifestations are simply the visible part. In spiritual matters it is the physical object or action (what we tend to think of as the "real") that becomes the symbol or the metaphor for the reality. Our understanding of this will develop as we go along.

"Oh, I see," someone will immediately say, "you're talking about the supernatural, something mystical!" No. This is one of the grave errors we fall into, especially in the West, which we will discuss in the next chapter. It hinders our understanding of the gospel and our learning to live in obedience and love. It helps us not at all to experience the existential realities of the gospel. Jesus *never* spoke of "natural" *vs.* "supernatural" (or "supranatural"), or of "rational" *vs.* "mystical." These are dichotomies derived from pagan philosophy, and they are devastating to right thinking about the gospel. He spoke simply about the "old" *vs.* the "new," and he said," Behold, I make all things new" (Revelation 21.5). That is what the gospel is all about, and sacraments – the passage, journey, pilgrimage from *old* to *new, the new being Jesus' kingdom,* a realm that is present here and now in our midst (because he brings it and we receive and experience it in the sacraments), but is also yet to come.

We are still *in* the world, yet the passage can and does take place. We live in two worlds. *The initial means of that passage is baptism,* of which *water* is the earthly, physical *symbol.* By obeying Jesus' command to submit to baptism, we begin our spiritual pilgrimage of obedience and start to grow in love. We submit to his Church and to her ministry to us in the sacrament of baptism, and begin to learn humility. Baptism was from the inception of the Church the mark of entry into it,the mark of commitment, the mark of *death to self* and the beginning of the *new life in Christ.* It is foreshadowed in the Old Testament by the passage of the Israelites through the Red Sea in their deliverance from Egypt on their way to the "Promised Land." (There are deep significances here: death to the old life, cleansing from sin, leaving the "flesh pots" of Egypt [Exodus 16.3] to achieve the promise of heaven, etc., which we cannot go into.) As we have noted earlier, death is for the Christian not the end but the beginning; it is our participation with Christ in his crucifixion, followed by our resurrection with him and entry into his kingdom which we celebrate in the Eucharist, as we will see.

There are those who believe, incidentally, that if they are baptized, then fall into sin, they will lose their salvation in Christ. Some in the time of the early Church believe this, so the put off baptism until the last possible moment. The Church, however, disapproved of this and taught that salvation is always possible through repentance and faith, for Jesus' grace is not limited. As John wrote, "If we confess our sins, he is faithful

and just, and will forgive our sins and cleanse us from all un-
righteousness" (1 John 1.9).

Thus, infant baptism was practiced from the beginning
of the Church in obedience to Jesus' words to Nicodemus,
" . . . unless one is born of water and the Spirit, he cannot enter
the kingdom of God" (John 3.5), and also, "Let the children
come to me, and do not hinder them; for to such belongs the
kingdom of God" (Luke 18.16). We spoke of baptism as a
"passage" or "journey." Infants have to be carried by their parents
(or surrogates) who make the baptismal vows on their behalf,
just as parents see to everything else about their welfare while
they are small. Denial of infant baptism is a late development,
introduced in the sixteenth century by a sect known as Anabap-
tists, meaning " those baptized again," because they denied the
validity of infant baptism and insisted on rebaptizing persons who
had been baptized as infants, on the assumption that baptism
requires a conscious declaration of faith. They removed the
mystery, but baptism consists, as do all the sacraments, of the
mystery of *God's action,* not ours only. It is "logical" to think
of it as merely a declaration of faith, but "logic" can be contrary
to Spirit, and the early Church was strong in spiritual understanding.

An analogy will perhaps make this clearer. Today babies are
immunized against small pox, diphtheria, polio and many other
diseases. We do not postpone the innoculations until they can
give their conscious consent. To those lacking scientific knowledge, the rituals of innoculation are a mystery; they simply have
faith that parents and doctors know what they are doing. One
day we will understand the efficacy of baptism as clearly as we
understand immunization, since we will understand "as we are
understood" (1 Corinthians 13.12). For now it remains a
mystery, a hidden reality. We are so deeply influenced by science
today that we are afraid of mystery in the Church. But the human
soul knows that the faith is a mystery, and if it is denied mystery
in the formal Church it will seek it elsewhere.

Eucharist

Jesus commanded at the Last Supper, after he has taken bread and blessed and broken it and given it to his disciples,"Take, eat; this is my body" (Matthew 26.26). Then he took a cup (of wine) saying, "Drink of it, all of you; for this is my blood . . ." (v. 27) The corresponding passages in Mark and Luke are almost identical with these. St. Paul writes (of the bread), "This is my body which is broken for you. Do this in remembrance of me" (1 Corinthians 11.24). And of the wine, "Do this, as often as you drink it, in remembrance of me" (v. 25).

This entire action, subsequently carried out by the disciples and by us today in obedience and love, is significant in the extreme. The realization was borne in upon the disciples that it signified the crucifixion (the broken body, the blood poured out), which was God's sacrifice for all mankind. It was the end of the Mosaic law, the end of the temple sacrifices of animals, the completion of the old covenant (agreement) God had made with Israel, which is set forth in the Old Testment. This, together with the resurrection, represented *pascha,* prefigured by the passage (Passover) when in Egypt the angel of death in Egypt "passed over" the homes of the Israelites sprinkled with blood of lambs, and the "first born" were thereby saved from death (there are again layers of significance here.). It represented and established transformation from the old to the new, the end of old, fallen Adam and the beginning of the reign of the New Adam, who is Christ. The blood now shed is Christ's instead of a lamb's; or, rather, *he* is the "lamb of God" (John 1.29) whose blood saves from death all who will receive it acknowledging its saving power.

This was the beginning of the new covenant (New Testament).It was the beginning of the "new creation," in which we participate, if we unite ourselves with Jesus in his death and resurrection by offering him ourselves. This is what happens in the Eucharist. It is, at minimum, the pivotal point of all history. It is also the pivotal point in every person's life. It is the passage from death into eternal life, which because of Christ is present here and now "in our midst" and is of a quality entirely different from that of temporal life, a quality that will be reflected in outward actions as well as inner experience. It is our passage from crucifixion of self (which we have already discussed) into resurrection with Christ and our ascension with him to the Father. Jesus' question to the Pharisees confronts us all: "What is your opinion about Christ" (Matthew 22.42 *P*)? That is, do we acknowledge *who he is?* No living person can escape answering it, for to refuse to answer is itself an answer. Here obedience and love must begin – or end. We need to comprehend this; otherwise we have not perceived what Jesus Christ and the Christian faith, and love and obedience, are all about.

Eucharist comes from the Greek word "thanksgiving." For when the Son of God has himself sacrificed his life to save us, what is left but for us to participate in that sacrifice, as he commanded, by a rite of celebration *in thanksgiving*? The Protestant preference is for "Communion," or "Holy Communion." In the Roman Church the rite is called the "Mass."[1] In any event, the Eucharist is a *corporate* action *by the Church.* For several people to go off by themselves with some bread and wine and say, "Now we're going to have a Eucharist," is nonsense, regardless of what prayers they may utter.

In all our discussions here, we will concentrate on the understanding of the Church up until A.D. 1054, the year of the "great schism" between East and West. We will thus be focusing on the experience and understanding of the one, *undivided Church* during the first 1,000 years of its existence.[2] This was the Church that produced scripture (as we will see in the next chapter) and lay closest in time and thought to our Lord and his Apostles.

It also took scripture with the utmost seriousness. When Jesus said, . . . "unless you eat the flesh of the Son of man and drink his blood, you have no life in you . . ." (John 6.53), they took it to mean exactly that. They did not require reconciliation of it with pagan Greek philosophy. God does what he will do, and if he determines that bread and wine taken and blessed and consumed according to a formula he prescribes *are* therefore his flesh and blood, he assuredly has the power to make them so. If this is offensive to some, or unbelievable, or unacceptable, or merely metaphorical, so it was also to many of Jesus' immediate disciples, and "After this many of his disciples drew back and no longer went about with him" (John 6.66). It was even more offensive to the "refined" Greek intellectuals, who regarded the Christians as a pack of cannibals. It is the extreme intimacy of the Eucharist that offends. In receiving the body and blood of our Lord in the Eucharist, we are partaking of an intimacy with God closer than that of our mothers and fathers when they conceived us. We don't like that. In our "sanitized" twentieth century we want our relationship to God "cleaned up" by being intellectualized. But the prolonged discourse of Jesus about his body and blood in John 6.25-71 admits of nothing but a straightforward interpretation, and the undivided Church was willing to grant God the mystery of it.

Let us continue now our discussion of the Eucharist.

We have spoken of the Church as "that which is called out." Its members are to be the "salt of the earth" – different, set aside for the special purpose of "seasoning" the whole world. We have spoken of the Christian's life being one of action in obedience to Christ, and this means to follow him from the old into the new, to be renewed by him, to be a "new creature" in him. As Saint Paul put it, " . . . if any one is in Christ he is a new creature; the old has passed away, behold, the new has come" (2 Corinthians 5.17). The Christian, then, is in a state of movement, procession, passage from the old way of death into the new Way of Life.

This is a movement of the spirit within us, but it has also external, physical manifestations. What are they? They begin with the action of going to Church. Sunday morning we get up, wash, and put on our best clothes, for who does not want to look his best when going to meet his beloved? The movement, procession, passage begins at the front door. We may not think of it that way; whether we walk or drive, the outward action may seem not much different from going shopping or anywhere else. But we reflect on it, we will perceive that this action has a very different quality about it. For we are leaving the "world," for an hour or so anyway, to be both visibly and inwardly members of the body "that is called out."

The early Church enacted this every Sunday, and oftener. They saw profound meaning in the fact that the corporate action began at the front door. The members moved to the house of worship as a body, praying and singing. This action is symbolically preserved today in the movement and processions we find in the liturgical churches.

Then there was the "entrance." Again, this was meaningful. The people were entering God's house, approaching his heavenly kingdom, which was a spiritual state but also represented physically by the "sanctuary" containing the altar, toward which the people faced, There was more prayer and responsive singing. Inside, there were no chairs and the people remained standing for the service, which might last for hours. Scripture was read and a sermon was preached.[3] With prayers of adoration, thanksgiving, praise, intercession and confession of unworthiness, preparation was made for the serving of the Eucharist and the receiving by the people of the body and blood of our Lord as he commanded.

Bread and wine, plain elements of our daily food from the people, were offered to God on the altar. Christ's words at the Last Supper proclaiming their transformation were recalled, and the blessing of the Holy Spirit invoked to accomplish the transformation of the bread and wine. It was God's action, not man's alone, and the Church did not require of God a "scientific" or "logical" explanation of what he was doing. Then the Eucharist was served to the people, and with the people it was sent out into the world. It was and is on the face of it all quite simple and ordinary.

Someone will immediately say, "If it's so simple and ordinary, why all the ceremony?" The answer is that it is also terribly *extraordinary*. There is mystery here and, as with so much in the Christian faith, paradox. Plain, ordinary people are involved, and plain, ordinary food is offered. Yet, by God's action in ordinary food and plain people, extraordinary changes occur. The earth trembles, and a *new creation appears in us and in the world!* That new creation is Christ, and we in him (2 Corinthians 5.17). If we have not seen and experienced this, then we have not yet seen and experienced what the Christian faith is all about. This is *liturgy,* a word, as we said in Chapter 4, derived from the same Greek roots that give us *layman* and *work. Liturgy is the work of man offering to God and receiving from him.*

Let us return for a moment to Jesus' words. He said, "Do this in remembrance of me," or "in memory of me." (Luke 22:19) But neither "memory" nor "remembrance" is satisfactory. The Greek word used by both Luke and Saint Paul (1 Corinthians 11.24,25) is *anamnesis* (a-nam'-ne-sis), and it implies far more than mere recollection or remembrance. It means to *bring foward into the present an experience of the past, making it a living reality now,* a reality that is no less actual and true for all its being a mystery. A possible translation of Jesus' words might even be, "Do this *when you wish to have me with you."* In no way, then, can the Eucharist be considered merely a "memorial service."

Whose experience of the past are we speaking of? The experience of the Church and of Jesus' disciples, stretching back in unbroken continuity to the Upper Room and the Last Supper. For the Church remembers and experiences *now,* as an individual cannot, since the Church is eternal; *in* time, it is tim*eless,* for it is also in eternity.[4] *This is why it is only by corporate action of the Church that we can receive Christ's body and blood as he commanded. It is in his Church that Christ gives us his body and blood now* just as he did his disciples in the Upper Room and on the cross. It is all *one and the same action.*

In celebrating the Eucharist we are like a man laying a fire; we prepare the paper and the wood, but we have no flame to ignite it. So God supplies the flame. If it were not so, the rite would be a vacant, meaningless exercise. We must remember the "tongues of flame" at Pentecost (Act 2.3) – the fire is always from God[5] (*cf.* 1 Kings 18.38; 1 Chronicles 21.26; 2 Chronicles 7.1; etc.). If we think about this we will see it. Jesus did not, like a philosopher, come and formulate some ideas for us to ponder, and then depart. Therefore "remembrance" and "memory" are not really suitable words. Jesus *acted* and commanded. He *made* a new creation in which he desires us to participate and in which we may participate by *obeying* the commands he left us. This is *God in action.* In this action God makes explicit and creates *as a present reality* his *kingdom of love,* a kingdom heretofore unknown, or known but dimly and at a distance. From here on we have no excuse for saying we do not know it and therefore cannot live in it, for *in Christ God has given it to us* (Luke 12.32).

Someone may ask, "Are we not then in celebrating the Eucharist crucifying Christ all over again?" No. What he did he did *in time once* for all (1 Peter 3.18). But his was also an *eternal* act, and he left us the formula for that act to be *repeatedly realized* (that is, made *fully real*) *in time,* and that formula is the formula of the Eucharist. This can never be understood or explained in terms of pagan logic or outward appearances. It can only be understood in the Spirit. We must not be fearful of this mystery, for it is the mystery of God himself. It does not mean either superstition or speculation, for the mystery of God has been declared to us by reliable witnesses (Paul, for example, in 1 Corinthians, Ephesians, Colossians, and 1 Timothy). It is a "given." We cannot analyze the "why," the "wherefore," or even the "how" of it, but only *experience* and *perceive* it. It is God's love presented to us, spread before us, and prepared to work within us. That being the case, we have to let God be God and do things *his* way. To have scruples based on the rationalizations of philosophy is to give in to the temptation to have it *our* way and eliminate the mystery.

This, then, is what *we do* in the sacrament of the Eucharist, and what *Christ does* for us as we meet him in it:

> We truly ascend to heaven and participate *now* in the kingdom that is both now and yet to come.[6] In this we are energized by the Holy Spirit to return in peace to the world and live in it empowered to obey Jesus's commands to love God, ourselves and our neighbors. Through us the Eucharist

returns to the world, and through the Eucharist the world is transformed.

Having earlier been baptized, we receive in the Eucharist Christ's life in us and are "born again" of the Spirit, "putting on" Christ.

Having "received the heavenly Spirit." (as is said in the eucharistic liturgy of John Chrysostom) and having been "born again," we can realize that Christ was, and is, indeed the life of the world, and that in killing him the world itself dies, and so will pass away. *Life is no longer the "pursuit of happiness"* according to our earthly desires and ambitions, but *life is death in Christ.*

We do not condemn the world, but we perceive that the world condemns Christ.

In the Eucharist we find passage from the life of this world with its sorrow, suffering and death into the *new life of joy in Christ.*

We recognize Christ as both the gift and the giver. He supplies all that we have to offer, then in obedience to the Father, and out of love for the Father and for us offers himself for us. Because he was fully obedient to the Father, his sacrifice and love are total, complete, perfect – the only such sacrifice ever made on earth, and the model for us to imitate, even though our sacrifice will ever be imperfect. (This is spelled out in the book of Hebrews.)

In the Eucharist we find the *empowerment* to be what God desires and means us to be, and that empowerment is from God.

We discover that all our earthly hunger, suffering and frustrations are not meaningless, because they are received and transformed by Christ. A "stupid life and a stupid death" are no longer inevitable, but life becomes purposeful because it has its end in Christ.

In the Eucharist we find our ultimate approach to God on earth. He meets us there through the grace of the Holy Spirit, whom the Father sends in Jesus' name – that is, in response to Jesus' action in the Eucharist (John 14.26).

In the Eucharist is the end of fear, anger, frustration, wrath, lusts, earthly desires, worry – every human passion, for Christ is the fulfillment of every desire.

In the Eucharist is reconciliation of men with God, and peace within themselves and with one another. In the face of Christ's present action (*anamnesis*), all the argument and discord fall away, and there is unity. This is why "peace" is a sustained theme in the liturgy of the Eucharist, for Jesus said, "Peace I leave with you . . ." (John 14.27). To witness the instant dropping away of conflict, both internal and external, at the foot of the cross in the Eucharist (as I have) is a very dramatic experience.

If all this seems strange and beyond our depth, we need to remenber that intellectually it can be but dimly apprehended, if at all. Jesus did not come leaving us a set of intellectual propositions. He acted, and left commands. Philosophical scruples avail nothing. The way to understand is to "taste and see" (Psalms 34.8).

However, in the light of what we have said thus far, we are now in a position to appreciate the meaning of "Church."

The Meaning of "Church"

We said at the beginning of this chapter that Church is "that place of the spirit in which we love Jesus, and obey him in love." So "Church" is first of all a spiritual matter. But, as we have seen, things of the spirit have their symbolic, and utilitarian, manifestations in the visible world. So, we can point down the street to a building, and someone will immediately think then that by "Church" we must mean that Methodist congregation, or Roman Catholic, or whatever. Or they may think of some hateful person they know who goes there and say to themselves, "Uh huh!" On the other hand, we can take words and try to formulate some sort of dictionary definition, but this is not satisfactory. What we really want to know is what *God* had in mind; what was Jesus thinking of when he said, " . . . on this rock [Greek *petra*] will I build my church . . . "? (Matthew 16.18) In a play on words he has just called Simon "Peter," meaning "rock," but the "rock" that is to be the foundation of the Church is assuredly Christ himself (1 Corinthians 10.4; 1 Peter 2.8), though Peter evidently is to be "first" among his followers, and closely identified with Christ. Also, Peter has just been the first to assert that Jesus is the Son of God (Matthew 16.16). So the "rock" may refer as well to that assertion, which is the "foundation" of the Church.

God has never permitted man to define "Church." *He* defines it, for it is his. Or, we may say that it cannot be defined in the sense of being encompassed in verbal meanings, for the Church is eternal and our words are temporal. Even the frequently used "body of Christ" means essentially nothing to someone who does not know the theological and historical background and has not experienced *Church in action.* We cannot, in fact, really know or understand or define or say much of anything about Church until we have *experienced* it.

This is a hard thing for us in these latter days in the West to understand. We are in love with verbal definitions. We are told over and over, "define your terms." We want reality all cut and dried and arrayed in neat categories. This derives from pagan Greek philosophy, the methods of which are hammered into us at all levels in school, whether we are aware of it or not. The result of applying these methods to Church is that a theological "idea" gets isolated from the main stream of total Christian experience, then someone founds a sect or new "denomination"on it and thus another fragment is broken off from the whole. This is scandalous, for Jesus prayed the Father that we all might be *one* as he and the Father are one (John 17.21). We will have more to say about this in the next chapter, for an appreciation of how the splintering of Christendom comes about is indispensable to gaining the wisdom we are seeking.

The Church from the beginning rested on the disciples' *experience* of Christ and of the baptism of the Holy Spirit at Pentecost. To be sure, there was a history of God's actions in the process of redeeming man, and it all hung together in a rational continuity, as Stephen eloquently showed in his trial before the Sanhedrin (Acts 7), but there is not a line of pagan Greek "logic" in the whole New Testament. When differences arose, they were tested, to see what was of God and what was not (1 John 4.1). The entire theology of the Church grew not from "ideas" but from its *experience in worship*. It would be well if we could return to that, but it is impossible now.[7] Too much has happened. What we *can* do, however, is *experience obedience to the commands of Jesus,* and in so doing *experience love* and *receive the rewards of love. Then* we will *know* Church in the only way it can be known on earth, and any other explanations or definitions will be superfluous.

Now, in the light of the above explanation and of all we have said thus far in this book, we are in a position to make some observations about what it means to be "the salt of the earth." From these we will be able to see the meaning of Church:

> The Church reveals itself as consisting of those who confess Jesus to be the Son of God (Romans 10.9). It is the place of our corporate adoration, praise and worship of the Father, Son and Holy Spirit.

> As we have seen, Jesus prayed the Father that the disciples might be one as (in exactly the same way that) he and the Father were one. That unity was expressed in *love and obedience* (John 5.30; 15.9). The unity of the Church is therefore a unanimity of action: obedience to Christ and love for God, ourselves, and for one another.

The Church is both the sign and the reality of God's love for us and of our reciprocated love in obedience to his Son.

Jesus said that Peter was the "rock" *(petra)* on which he would build his Church, and we noted that the "rock" was Christ himself, yet there was something in particular that caused Jesus to say that. It was *love*. The one disciple who fervently proclaimed his love for Jesus was Peter (John 21.15-17). The basis of the Church, the "rock" on which it is founded, is love.

The Church has been called the "family of God," of which Jesus is the head. The family is the Church in miniature, of which the father is the head, standing in Jesus' stead as priest. Both are arenas of obedience and love and deification. (see p. 32).

Church requires no logical or practical justification, however much secular sociology may call it "useful." It was created by God, and death itself cannot prevail over it (Matthew 16.18). The world cannot be in any way a standard for the Church, but the Church is the standard for the world.

The Church is not a set of doctrines but the showing forth of the work of God.

The Church is the *mystery* of the New Creation, the presence of the kingdom of heaven here and now in our midst.

The Church is *not* an institution or an organization, least of all an institution among other institutions. Forms of polity do not define the Church. Rather, the Church is an *event:* God in us and we in him, the epiphany of love.

Church is the *experience* of the new state of being wrought by Christ.

Church is not the practice of "religion" or the presence of religion or the place of "religious" activity. It is the *end of religion.*[8]

Church is the place of *movement* from the world into the kingdom and back again (this is the meaning of "liturgy"), bringing Christ and his kingdom with us *for the world.*

It is the place where we receive the body and blood which Christ consecrated by his victorious surrender in death to *give us life.*

Church is mission and hope for the world: Christ acting in us.

Church is the world that has died and been resurrected, then reborn.

The Church is the place where we receive support, encouragement and direction in our Christian battles – the "violence" we spoke of in Chapter 3. It is the home of repentant, and forgiven, sinners.

The Church is the scene of the Way of Life in a world that is dying.

Church is the redemption and sanctification of time – that which gives it meaning and purpose, the end toward which it is proceeding. Without the Church, time is a pointless treadmill, ours a "stupid life and a stupid death."[9]

Church is the place where, before God, we mutually forgive all that we have ever held against one another at any time, and in turn receive God's forgiveness of our offences against him.

Church is the place where alienation ends. It is the place of reconciliation among men and of all things in Christ.

The Church is the place where our offerings (about which we will say much more in the last chapter) are ultimately accepted and ratified by God – or rejected.

The Church is the "bride"of Christ (Revelation 21.9). Every husband is to love his wife "as [in the very same way that, to the precise degree that] Christ loved [and loves] the Church and gave himself up for her" (Ephesians 5.25).

The Church is that body to which the sacraments ordained by Christ are committed by him for the accomplishment of his mission on earth.[10]

The Church as the New Creation on earth, is the Israel of God (Galatians 6.16). It is the *kingdom* realized here and now imperfectly, but yet to come in its full perfection.

This list is far from exhaustive, but it is sufficient to give us an appreciation of what Church is all about, and why loving the Church is an act of obedience to Christ. This obviously does not mean that our parishes and congregations are without flaw. The Church is, still, *in* the world, and the world invades it in many ways, which we will discuss in the next chapter, yet it is also the manifestation of the kingdom to which we as Christians belong and which we serve in love.

Notes

[1]"Mass is a word derived from the ending of the eucharistic rite when it was celebrated in Latin. The priest said, "*Ite, missa est,*" which means, "Go, it is sent." Most people thought it meant, "Go, the mass (service) is ended." What it meant was that the Eucharist was sent out with the people as a gift to the world, which is one of the basic understandings of the significance of the Eucharist.

[2] It may seem wildly inaccurate to speak of the Church before A.D. 1054 as "undivided" when over the centuries there were quarrels innumerable. Alexandria, for example, was given to finding an excess of symbolism in scripture. However, there was (and still is) a body of "Orthodox" beliefs, based on scripture and the decisions of the seven great ecumenical councils, to which all Christians can rally, and to which indeed they must return as a foundation if ever Christendom is to be re-united. It is to this pre-A.D. 1054 Orthodoxy that we are referring when we speak of the undivided Church. Actually, A.D. 1054 is merely the date of the formal East/West break. Before that, the philosophical tide that was increasingly engulfing the West, and which we will examine in the next chapter, repeatedly washed back to the East using disruptions and profound misunderstandings.

[3] In most Protestant denominations the sermon (proclamation of the word) is the focus of the service, and the Bible is prominent. It is often incorrectly assumed that other churches neglect scripture reading and the sermon. In the undivided Church, of which we are writing, scripture was always read, and the sermon had a prominent place. In the Great Church in Antioch, for example, in the time of St. John Chrysostom (perhaps the greatest preacher who ever lived – his name means "golden-mouthed"), the Sunday sermon was an hour or more long, and often there were two of them!

[4] The Church is *one*, and *eternal*. Thus all Christians who ever lived are as much part of the Church *now* as we are. In the Church, properly understood, there is no dividing line between "then" and "before" and "now" and "hereafter." In the Church is eternal contemporaneity and we live in the company of all the saints, surrounded by them who are a "cloud of witnesses" (Hebrews 12.1).

[5] The offering of bread and wine is also acknowledged as being from God. In the words of the liturgy, "Thine own of thine own we offer unto thee . . ."

[6] Those who are familiar with his writings will recognize in this and the following section, as well as throughout this chapter, my indebtedness to the late Father Alexander Schmemann, Dean of St. Vladimir's Seminary, Crestwood, N.Y.

[7] No sooner had I written that it was impossible to return to a theology based on the experience of worship than I was shown a book by Geoffrey Wainwright, *Doxology: the Praise of God in Worship, Doctrine and Life* (New York, 1980). The author writes that the book "is primarily intended as a systematic theology written from a liturgical perspective. It can also be considered as a theology of worship." He is a Methodist, and Professor of Systematic Theology at the Divinity School of Duke University. It is very much in the spirit of the undivided Church.

[8] It is "the end of religion" because after Christ there is nothing more. He is the Alpha and the Omega, the first and the last, the beginning and the end. (Revelation 22.13). To say one is "religious" can mean anything – a practioner of voodoo, or humanism, or Buddhism, or whatever. The secular world (which includes those who take polls) does not understand this and counts obedience to Jesus Christ as simply "another religion."

[9] The Church is in fact the determinant of history. In a most significant paper, Charles Malik has written, "Without the given, existing, continuing church, whether in the form of the first church, which is the people of God, ancient Israel, or the new church, which is the Body of Christ, there is no history." ("History-Making, History-Writing, History-Interpreting," in *Center Journal* [Notre Dame, Indiana, Center for Christian Studies, Fall, 1982], p.38.) In other words, without the eternal Church, in which is our eternal life, "history" is precisely nothing, a meaningless rigmarole, a "sound and fury" going nowhere and signifying nothing.

[10] Some churches have moved far away from the early Church's firm understanding of the efficacy of baptism and the Eucharist. A prominent U.S. pastor has written, "Sacramentalism is ever a curse to the preaching as the believing of the true gospel. The ordinances [baptism, Eucharist, etc.] are not sacraments; they are not the means and the channels of saving grace." (W.A. Criswell, *Criswell's Guidebook for Pastors* [Broadman Press, 1980], p. 201, quoted in *Again*, publication of the Evangelical Orthodox Church, Isla Vista, California, Vol. 6, No.2) The pagan philosophical influence, which we will discuss in the next chapter, is quite evident here.

Chapter Eleven

WE SERVE HIS CHURCH IN LOVE

How do we find love and make it the center of our lives? By obeying the commands of Jesus; in so doing we become like him, adopted brothers and sisters of his, united with him in love, and united with him in obedience to the Father, who *is* love itself. That is what this book has been all about.

We introduced in the preceding chapter the context in which all this takes place. It is a set of personal inter-relationships, a "co-inherence," among those who have united themselves with Christ, and it is called *Church*. As we have said, in the Christian life individualism is out. Revelation from God *always* come in the context of Church, for the Church is *his*, as we have seen. Any individual claiming revelation privately apart from the Church is properly viewed with extreme skepticism until his (or her) understanding is confirmed by the experience of the Church as a whole – the entire body of Christ. That is not to say that God does not act upon individuals. He confers differing gifts upon each of us, but we are above all *one body*, as Saint Paul eloquently sets forth in the 12th chapter of 1 Corinthians (then immediately in the 13th chapter shows us the "still more excellent way," which is love.) Even the Christian recluse knows this, for it was the first monk, Saint Anthony of Egypt, who lived in a cave in the desert, who said, "Your life and your death are with your neighbor."

The skeptic will say, "You mean all this that you have been describing happens in *Church*?" The question arises only because we have so little understansing of what *Church* means. The answer is, "yes" – to the extent that the body calling itself "Christian" is *being* Church, for "Church" is not defined by a set of words but by what God *does* in the body and by what its members do in their inter-relationships as a body in *obedience* to God. Remember that Church is *ekklesia* – "those who have been called out." that is, *from the world.* To the extent that there is any love or obedience to God in the world, it is because love has "infected" it. To the extent that there is *lack* of love and obedience *in the Church,* it is because the Christian body has been "infected" by the world. We are, as we must constantly remember, "the salt of the earth" – that by which the world is changed. We dare not lose our "saltness."

"Church" is therefore the summation of love and obedience – of everything about which we have spoken in this book. And *the Church is one.* This especially we must understand, for Jesus prayed, and *insists,* that *we be one.* Nor are Jesus' prayers futile. They are cosmically effective, proclaiming the order of the universe. We buck them only to our own destruction. Therefore, let us take careful note of what Jesus said in the great dominical prayer in John 17.20-23:

> I do not pray for these only, but also for those who are to believe in me through their word, *that they may all be one; even as* [in the same way that] thou, Father, art in me, and I in thee, that they also may be in us, so that the world may believe that thou hast sent me. The glory which thou hast given me I have given to them, *that they may be one even as* [in the same way that] *we are one,* I in them and thou in me, *that they may become perfectly one,* so that the world may know that thou hast sent me and hast loved them even as [in the same way that] thou hast loved me.

In precisely what manner were Jesus and the Father "one"? One in essence, certainly , as the Nicene creed states, and also *in mutual love* and in Jesus' *total obedience to the Father.* We also as Christians are therfore to be one in love for one another and in our obedience to the Father through Christ. There is a difference, however. It occurs because we are fallen creatures and the Father and the Son are not. We sin against God and against one another (that is, we violate the command to love, sin being a breach of love), and the Father and Son do not. The sin can be "covered," the breach healed over, only by asking for and receiving forgiveness from God and from one another. This is a necessity, and Jesus has already commanded it, as we saw in Chapter 4. Without mutual forgiveness (God's forgiveness of us and our forgiveness of one another) the unity of love cannot take place. What this implies with respect to our present division in Christendom we will discuss under "Offerings." First, let us continue to enlarge our understanding of "Church" as the context in which we learn and practice love and obedience.

* * * * *

"Church"is mentioned only twice in the gospels, once when Jesus tells Peter he is the "rock" on which he will build his Church (Matthew 16.18), and once when he instructs his disciples to go to a sinful brother and tell him his fault and if he will not listen then to tell it to the Church (Matthew 18.17). In the rest of the New Testament, however, it is mentioned over 100 times. Obviously, for the early Christians the Church was the center of the Way of Life, the embodiment of all that it meant to be a Christian, and Jesus clearly intended it to be so.

Jesus also clearly meant his Church to be the creature of the Holy Spirit, whom he would send to initiate, guide and sustain it. (The Church, we remember, began at Pentecost with the descent of the Holy Spirit, as told in Acts 2.) It is in the Church, therefore, both visibly in our relationships to others and invisibly within ourselves, that we find the summation of the Christian's life of obedience in love and of love in obedience.

Thus in a glorious mutuality, the "Grand Co-inherence" that we spoke of in Chapter 9, we are to serve the Church, and in it our fellow man, just as Christ loves and serves his Church because it is his "bride" (Revelation 21.9), and through it loves and serves us. The implications of this for our attitudes and for what we do in our lives, and for what the Church does under the guidance of the Holy Spirit, are far-reaching.

what we do in our lives, and for what the Church does under the guidance of the Holy Spirit, are far-reaching.

The Watchful Christian

We noted earlier that we live today in a pagan world, just as did the early Christians. It is hostile to Christ and to his Church. In such a situation, what attitude is a Christian and his Church to hold?

Jesus furnishes the answer in his commands to *watch!*

Why watch? Because *love is always watchful.* It watches with the eyes of God; our watchfulness is the watchfulness of love.

What are we to watch for?

For Jesus' return, for one thing. In his discourse in Mark 13 on "signs of the end" Jesus foretells that he will return as "master of the house" (his Church), but no one knows when that will be, not even the angels nor Jesus himself, but only the Father (Mark 13.32). There are similar passages in Matthew 24 and 25 in Luke 12 and 21.

Jesus does come to us at various times and in various ways, and there will surely be a climactic ultimate return. We are to be alert and watchful *at all times* for his touch, his word, his summons, his quiet command by which he communicates his will to us. Meanwhile we have also to watch against temptations to sin.

There is a clue to how we must watch in the scene in the Garden of Gethsemane on the night when Jesus was betrayed. He went apart with Peter, James and John and commanded them to *watch* with him (Matthew 26.38). Going a little farther he fell on his face and prayed, and Luke (the physician) mentions that "his sweat became like great drops of blood" (Luke 22.44). When he returned he found the disciples sleeping, and he said to Peter, " . . . could you not watch with me one hour? *Watch and pray that you may not enter into temptation . . .*" (Matthew 26.40,41). Here is a foreshadowing of the situation in the "end times" described by Jesus in Mark 13.34-37. Peter, the "doorkeeper," (of the Church, the kingdom) was commanded to watch, and instead he slept. Peter also will presently deny Jesus three times. From what Jesus says, the presumption is that if he had stayed awake and prayed he might have avoided those denials. Peter is the prototype of us all.

The cynic will interrupt here, saying, "Aw, come on! God sees everything and does it all anyway. Why bother to watch? Life is just hard work. Grab your sleep when you can."

God does see everything. He forgets not even a sparrow, and he knows every hair on our heads (Luke 12.6,7). He said, "I will never fail you nor forsake you" (Hebrews 13.5). But if God is so concerned about us, why is he so quiet? Why doesn't he shout at us, like some of the TV preachers? The answer is that there is a divine reticence, a courtesy that will not intrude upon us. His is a "still small voice" (1 Kings 19.12). God respects our privacy. We can be grateful for this, for otherwise, being omnipotent, he would be intolerable – an absolute tyrant. At the same time, he has taken us into his enterprise and given us work to do, and one of our jobs is to *watch!* We are to be sentinels both in the Church and at the door of our own hearts, watching against invasion of the Church by the world and against our own temptations to sin.

In a special way that involves prayer. The great teachers of the Church have always posited a connection between watchfulness and prayer. Colliander writes: "Prayer and watchfulness are one and the same, for it is with prayer that you stand at the gate of your heart. The watchful eye reacts immediately to the slightest shifting in the field of vision; so also does the heart that is steadfast in prayer. Like a spider watching for a fly to enter its web, . . . prayer watches in the middle of your heart; as soon as a trembling makes it known that an enemy is there, prayer kills it."[1]

We said in Chapter 8 that when we go forth as Christians in obedience to Jesus' commands we are plunged into a jungle. The world assaults us. Empty, secular pleasures try to seduce us into believing they are the *only* good. Satan comes at us. Against all this, our only protection is to *watch and pray* as Jesus commanded. The years of a Christian are a lifelong vigil. Watchfulness is necessary because hour by hour, sometimes from moment to moment, the Christian has to *choose* between good and evil, and when one is dealing with a brilliant and handsome deceiver like Satan, that choice requires keen perceptions. In their unfallen states Adam and Eve knew nothing of evil. After "their eyes were opened" (Genesis 3.7) they knew good *and* evil. So it has been since. One does not perceive and choose while sleeping. *Watchfulness is necessary to make choice possible.* It is far more profitable than speculation about prophecy.

Have you ever met a truly watchful Christian? You will find one in a dedicated monastic. There is a collectedness about them. They are reserved, almost shy. They are not taken in by posturing; they will not buy your act. They are on guard against the ingenuities of self-love, and their spiritual perceptions are honed to the point where they can spot these instantly in themselves – and in you. That is why you may feel uncomfortable in their presence. At the same time, you sense in them the "real thing," and it isn't Coke.

In sum, obedient love is watchful. As in so many aspects of the Christian faith, we may discover a lesson in a simple, everyday phenomenon. Consider a loving mother and her small child. Whatever she may be doing, she is watchful of the child with all her senses, which are quite a few more than the obvious five. A secret intuition tells her when he is in trouble, and a special sense in her heart knows when he is happy, and rejoices. We are to be like that, in imitation of God, who is watchful of us. He wants us to watch for the involuntary inward and outward gestures of indulgent self-love; watch especially for the inner and outer needs of our neighbor and fellow Christians; watch to keep ourselves obedient in love; and watch tor the coming of our Lord. In so doing we, too, can become the "real thing."

The Church Neglects to Watch

The Church also must, as a body, *watch*. The temptation is let its life be engulfed by worldly understanding, to let secular ideas overshadow the gospel.

That brings us to "philosophy," A word we will use in the sense of intellectual speculations apart from the revelation of scripture and the experience of Christian worship. It includes contemporary non-Christian "ideologies," and, inevitably, much of modern "psychology" and "sociology." We will be especially concerned, however, with classical Greek philosophies, which we will call "pagan'" because the Church had to compete against them for ultimate loyalty of the people, and still does. They invaded the Church, just as modern philosophies have invaded the Church today.

This is a sensitive subject, because there are many in our churches who would like to arrive at accommodations with various forms of paganism. Why bring it up? Because it has to do with love and obedience to Christ. In particular it has to do with the failure of love in the world and of love and obedience to Christ in much of the Church. Our pagan culture keeps infiltrating the Church and driving out love. It is not unlike a virus invading a cell and saying in effect, "*I* am in charge here; *I* will dictate what goes on." But this destroys the fullness, the "wholeness" ("health," for that is what "wholeness"means) of the Church. Let us consider therefore how the Church has managed its encounters with secular philosophy, and watched, or failed to watch.

* * * * *

When the Church after Pentecost began its mission, it was thrust into a Greek culture and compelled to use the Greek language, which was the universal language of the civilized world at that time. Classical Greek philosophy was the respectable way of thought, and the Christians with their strange talk of eating flesh and drinking the blood of their leader could hardly be considered respectable. (Before going any further, we should note that that is still pretty much the case today. All sorts of secular "philosophies," Greek in spirit, hold the edge in respectability. They are fully accepted and even accorded honor in our schools. Jesus is an outcast, specifically *excluded by law* from our public schools. He is also in the teaching of some "churches" merely peripheral – at best a "help," a mere "example.") But philosophy knows nothing of love, and the modern

philosophies that speak of "love" know only a parody of the real
thing. To the Christian, love, the real love that is found only
in Christ, is everything. We can begin now to see the dimen-
sions of the problem, how appalling it is.

This is not to denigrate the Greek language or Greek philosophy. God created them both for his purpose – the communica-
tion of the gospel. The problem is one of priority: is classical
philosophy and its spirit to "judge" and determine the gospel?
Or is human thought a "fallen" thing along with man himself
and, like all the rest of creation, awaiting redemption? The Christian answer is that Jesus Christ is the redeemer and "baptizer"
of all things, including philosophy. *He* is its judge; it does not
judge him or his words. We can begin to see how modern secular
thought has reversed this.

The best of the early Christian thinkers understood the problem. They were thoroughly educated in classical thought, and
they used that thought and its terminology to formulate Christian theology and communicate it to the civilized world of their
time, as God surely meant that they should. Basil the Great,
Gregory of Nyssa, and Gregory the Theologian, for example,
who are known as the Cappadocian Fathers, and others like
them "baptized" classical thought into the greater truth, the ultimate truth that is Jesus Christ. This occurred in the Eastern
Mediterranean for the most part, which was the center of the
civilized world, the seat of Empire being Constantinople. Development of Christian thought in the West would be different, as
we will see in a moment.

In spite of the work of the Fathers, however, heresies, which
are erroneous theology derived mainly from pagan philosophies
– falsification of the faith – kept erupting and had to be refuted
and excluded from the Church. Some, however, had strong
appeal, and we see many of them today in various cults and
sects. Strictly speaking, there are *new* heresies.

For, example, the dominant pagan philosophy at the time
of the early Church was Platonism, or more accurately, Neoplatonism, a reformulation of the thought of Plato (d. 347 B.C.),
which posited an eternal reality of "ideal" forms, of which earthly

creatures and other phenomena are temporary and imperfect reflections. Plato also posited an eternal "soul" in man that existed before he was born and would return to its eternal source.

It was very tempting to try to reconcile this with the Christian doctrine of resurrection and heaven, but it cannot be done. For one thing, the Bible posits no "eternal soul" but speaks of the resurrection of the *body*. When "soul" is mentioned in the New Testament there is always the presumption of its being associated with a body. Christianity knows nothing of a disembodied "soul."

But Platonism is so "idealistic," so "spiritual"; doesn't it really amount to the same thing as Christianity? Well, if you are willing to concede that Jesus never really, physically died for our sins, never shed real blood, and that he was just "great moral teacher"; or, if you will opt for an "idealized,"dehumanized, "spiritualized," sanitized, sterilized, "etherealized" Christ, then you may arrive at something that will square with Plato, but it will not be the Christ of the gospel.

One can see the appeal this would have to the "high-minded" Greek intellectuals. A sublimated Christ they might accept, for they were always open to "something new" (Acts 17.21). The cross was, however, to them foolishness (1 Corinthians 1.23). So, two things happened: heresies sprang up; and some otherwise brilliant and accurate Christian teachers adopted the pagan alternative on certain crucial points. Origen of Alexandria, for example, (d. A.D. 253) "was quite willing to acknowledge . . . that he shared the doctrine of the immortality of the soul with pagan philosophers."[2] The Second Council of Constantinople (A.D. 553) condemned his teaching.

Another appealing aspect of Plato was his making man the seeker after God, thus letting man feel important because he can pride himself on taking the initiative. But the Christian understanding is that the initiative is from God; *it is God who seeks us.* This is humbling, and it makes the pagan uncomfortable, for he does not wish to be "found out," as he is when God finds him and reveals his impotence and his willful wickedness. Yet Neoplatonism remains very much on the scene still today, even in some churches.

In the period of the undivided Church of which we have been

speaking (before A.D. 1054) the major intellectual centers were, as we said, in the East – Alexandria, Antioch and Constantinople, and the pagan philosophy most influential in theology was, as said, Neoplatonism. The ideas of Aristotle were also having some influence, but nothing like the influence they were about to have in the West. In the end, the Church in the East, in great wisdom, settled on a theology derived from worship in which the Holy Spirit was clearly present. (See Note 7, Chapter 10.) This was a theology focused on God and *God's action in worship*. It became the theology of Orthodoxy, and remains so today.

Meanwhile, in the West, there developed an entirely different relationship between classical (pagan) Greek philosophy and the Christian faith as revealed in scripture. Since we today, whether Roman Catholic or Protestant, are still profoundly under the influence of that development it is important for us to recognize and understand it.

At the time when the Fathers in the East were formulating Christian doctrine based on scripture, but using the Greek language and philosophical terminology, Italy and most of Europe was predominantly barbarian. It knew very little of Greek philosophy. Even the great St. Augustine knew hardly any Greek. The language was Latin, and the tradition was Roman, which was very legalistic in spirit.

Then, in the Medieval period following the Dark Ages, Greek philosophy burst into Western Europe, carried by the Arabs, who had translated Aristotle. Aristotle appealed to the legalistic spirit of the Church in the West, and it seized upon Aristotle as a means to make the gospel "rational."[3] Thinkers such as Thomas Aquinas used Aristotelian logic to "prove" the existence of God and to set forth Christian doctorine. Theirs came to be known as the "scholastic method." It introduced a spirit of legalism and rigid secular rationality into the Church and shaped Christian understanding in a way quite alien to that of the gospels. It led to defining the faith in terms of "categories" and intellectual "propositions," and to trying to find God in the rationalities of Greek "scientific method." In short, it tried to arrive at

"God in a box" of secular understanding. The method was similar to that of an anatomist studing an organism: dissect it, identify its component elements, analyze them, comment on them, develop theories about them. The end result is dead – a dismembered corpse. The method is also deadly to the living gospel.[4]

All this was, unfortunately, not just a passing aberration. It came to be accepted by many that the gospel must pass under the scrutiny of science.[5] Or, since science was "neutral" and universal, it might be made the basis of a "universal religion," a new revelation supplanting the gospel. This idea emerged in at least one concrete form, namely Communism – "scientific socialism." It is with us as well in a powerful syncretist movement that would meld all faiths into one universal "brotherhood of man," submerging the gospel. But if the gospel is truth, syncretism has to be a lie.

In the West, then, the spirit of Hellenistic thought overshadowed the gospel. *This was just the opposite of the spirit of the Eastern Fathers* who, while using the terminology of Greek philosophy, transformed it utterly by "baptizing" it into the "higher wisdom" of Christ. Thus was philosophy "redeemed" by Christ. The West, however, proceeded to "de-baptize," to "unredeem" philosophy by setting its rationalities above those of the gospel.

Many instances of this difference could be enumerated. One or two here can only give us an inkling of what they are like. As scripture tells us, and as we saw in Chapter 10, Jesus was quite insistent in saying of the bread and wine in the Eucharist, "This *is* my body . . . my blood . . . " Saint Paul said that kind of talk was "foolishness" to the Greeks (1Corinthians 1.23) as indeed it was, for they were very "rational" by secular standards. The Eastern Fathers were content to take what Jesus said at face value, assuming, as Paul did, that the "foolishness of God is wiser than men . . . " (v. 25). The Roman West, however, wanted a "logical"explanation, and applying dialectic reasoning came up with "transubstantiation." Subsequently, some Protestant bodies, including ones who profess allegiance to "scripture only," went still futher in applying "rational" thought and said in effect, "But the Greeks were quite right. They just did not understand that Jesus was speaking only figuratively. He did not mean us to be cannibals! The Eucharist has no present reality. It is just a service in memory of Christ's death." Thus they subject the plain words of scripture to the plausibilities of Greek secular rationality.

Or, to cite another example: A prominent Orthodox theologian writes, "The truths of the faith are truths of experience, truths of fact."[6] A Protestant may answer, "Indeed not! The truths of the faith are *principles* for us to learn from scripture by word and example, then apply. Anything else is just mystical." The influence of Hellenic thought here is very marked. What does not conform to its canons is "mystical," "irrational," "anti-intellectual" – all pejorative terms. But it is Jesus Christ who is the truth, and he is the lord of *all,* including rational thought. *He is in very truth the standard of all rationality.*

This is a highly complex and difficult subject for us, because we are so deeply schooled in Greek rationalism, especially the syllogistic reasoning of Aristotle. This has far-reaching consequences of which we can suggest only a few. "Mind" became separated from "spirit" instead of their being *one* in the wholeness of the *person.* And instead of our attention being focused on the *unity of God and man in the one person Jesus Christ,* it remained, in the Greek spirit , focused on man alone. The result was the Renaissance and "humanism," and later the "Enlightenment," God being far off in the distance somewhere, or dispensed with altogether.[7] Renaissance art, for example, glorifies the human form. In the East, however, which "transfigured" Greek thought, Christian art took the form of icons, which make nothing of the human form but seek to express the wonder of *man taken up and transfigured by God, dwelling with him in his kingdom.* (To Western eyes, so accustomed to naturalistic representations, icons may seem "primitive" or distorted, but the painters had mastered naturalistic forms before they even attempted icons. They knew exactly what they were doing.) Perception of the truth in the icon is a matter of "he who has eyes to see." But God never denies that perception to anyone who truly seeks it and asks to be given it.

This wide difference in perception is still manifest in much of our life today, but it was and is especially acute in theology. In the Orthodoxy that emerged in the East, theology was, as we said, based on the *action of God* in the liturgies of worship. In the West it rested on a cerebral exercise applying the methods of pagan classical philosophy in an attempt to make the gospel rational by secular standards.[8] Theology became a speculative "head trip" rather than the exposition of God's action among men. Today the secular ideas being introduced into the Church from so many directions (counsels of pragmatism, such as divorce and abortion, various "psychologies," and all sorts of opportunistic schemes and rationalizations that subvert the gospel) have their precedent in the introduction of pagan Greek philosophy a thousand years ago.[9] But in all these philosophies, so new and yet so old, *there is nothing of obedience to God and love,* only expedient rationalizations in the spirit of paganism. Yet it is *only in love that Christ makes all things new,* and *that* is the Christian faith.

In sum, the East by and large *watched* against the blandishments of secular Hellenistic thought. Theologians in the West not only neglected to watch against the intrusions of pagan classical thought into the realm of Christian revelation but repeatedly welcomed them. This can, and did, generate a certain arrogance of mind and wild speculation such as those of the nineteenth century philosopher "theologians." It fosters pride and self-love and an inordinate faith in the power and authority of words and of human mind apart from God. With respect to God it stresses the *cataphatic,* his "knowableness" (we think, if we speculate long enough about him). The early Fathers of the East, on the other hand, in greater humility, stressed the *apophatic* – that God is essentially "unknowable."

*   *   *   *   *

Let us recapitulate now some of the differences between the pagan and the Christian, so that we may be sharply aware of them, and *watch!*

For the Christian, Christ has conquered death. For the pagan, death is the end. (Platonic absorption into some "universal soul" is not at all what the Christian means by eternal life in Christ.)

For the Christian, the *person* is of eternal worth and retains his identity in "eternal life." In the eternity of the pagan, the person vanishes.

The Christian petitions God for others and regards himself as secondary. The pagan petitions only for fullillment of his own desires.

The Christian prays to God, "*Thy* will be done." The pagan prays, "*My* will be done."

The Christian trusts God's grace without demanding visible evidence. The pagan looks for omens.

The Christian perceives the work of the enemy, Satan, and resists. The pagan knows no such enemy.

For the Christian, love is the center of his life. The pagan has no doctrine of love.

The Christian knows he has been saved by Christ. The pagan doesn't know that he needs to be saved.

The pagan is constantly *seeking* for God. The Christian does not seek for God but knows himself to have been *found by God,* for Jesus came "to seek and to save the lost"(Luke 19.10).

The Christian desires the kingdom of God (Matthew 6.33). The pagan knows nothing of any such kingdom.

The pagan, in an intellectual "head trip," tries to apply secular logic to knowledge of God. The Christian knows the *person* of Jesus Christ to be "logic" of God.

The pagan tries to live exclusively by all sorts of earthly rationalities. The Christian lives by the ultimate rationality of Jesus Christ and his words, which will never pass away (Matthew 24.35). Knowledge, philosophy, and all man-made works will pass away, but not love (1 Corinthians 13.8-10).

These are but a few of the differences.

Thus did the Church in the West neglect to watch as it should have, even though Saint Paul had warned in his letter to the Church at Colossae; "Be careful that nobody spoils your faith through intellectualism ["philosophy" in RSV] or high-sounding nonsense. Such stuff is at best founded on men's ideas of the nature of the world, and disregards Christ!" (Colossians 2.8 *P*)

Let us look now at what happened when the Church *did* watch.

The Church Watches and Discerns

In contrast to the neglect of the Church in the West to watch and guard sufficiently against pagan philosophies, the Church did watch and act effectively with respect to scripture.

The Church antedates the New Testament. This is obvious on the face of it, for many passages in the New Testament speak about the Church, which came into being before so much as a line of the New Testament had been written.

The oldest writings in the New Testament are the epistles of Saint Paul to the already existent Church. At about the same time, however, many of the disciples began writing down their recollections of Jesus and what they had gleaned from others. Some of it was pretty accurate. Much of it was legend, which included a lot of pretty dubious stuff. It became evident to the Church that a compilation of writings that could be regarded as authentic would be needed. A modern biblical authority explains what happened:

. . . with the late first and early second-century prolifera-
tion of Christian and quasi-Christian literature, and with the
rise of heretical movements claiming apostolic authority,
many early fathers of the Church began to call for the for-
mation of a canonical collection of "New Testament" scrip-
tures. To be considered as canonical, a document had to
pass three tests: (1) it had to have been written by an apostle of by an immediate disciple of an apostle; (2) it had to
be recognized as authentic by at least one leading eccle-
siastical community in the ancient Church; and (3) it had
to be consistent with apostolic doctrine – that is, with the
rule of faith preserved in the living tradition of the
Church.[10]

There was a fair amount of dispute over what should and
should not be included. The four gospels were easily agreed
upon, together with the book of Acts, the letters of Saint Paul,
and 1 Peter and 1 John. There was hesitation over Hebrews,
James, 2 and 3 John, Jude and Revelation. In a pastoral letter
in A.D. 367, Athanasios of Alexandria declared the 27 books
we now have to be "exclusively canonical," and this was ratified
by a Council of bishops in Carthage in A.D. 397. So in the end,
the *tradition of the Church* gave us the New Testament as we
know it. Those today who adhere to "scripture only" owe more
to Church tradition than they realize.[11]

The power of the Holy Spirit is in the Church when it is being careful, discriminating and *watchful.* The power of the Spirit
is in scripture *through the historic Church* created by the Holy
Spirit at Pentecost.

We turn now in our last chapter to consider love and obedience in the living Church as we experience it today. A con-
venient way to look at this is to view our actions as "offerings"
to God, to his Church and to one another. Finally, we will take
heed of warnings and commmands Jesus has given for all churches in all times.

Notes

[1] *Colliander, The Way*, p. 58.

[2] Jaroslav Pelikan, *The Christian Tradition*, Vol. 1, *The Emergence of the Catholic Tradition*, (Chicago, 1971), p.48.

[3] A monumental work on the influence of the Aristotelian on Western thought, though written from an entirely secular standpoint, is: Alfred Korzybski, *Science and Sanity: an Introduction to Non-Aristotelian Systems and General Semantics*, 2nd ed., Lakeville, Connecticut, 1941). Our discussion of "pagan influence" is not intended to denigrate "reason" or secular culture as such. These obviously have their function in God's plan and on their merits can be morally, intellectually and esthetically defensible. As scripture shows, and we trust this book has borne out, ordinary reason and common sense are ever a Christian necessity. Our criticism is of those philosophies that would claim a religious commitment from us, or subordinate the gospel to their own methods and conclusions. To assume that we must defer to Aristotle because he formulated *the* laws of thought is a serious mistake. He formulated a *limited verbal-logical system*. It is as inadequate for rationalizing the gospel as is Newton's physics, for example, in explaining electricity.

[4] When the gospel presentation becomes deadened with philosophy, so great is the human thirst for the authentic original that ways are sought to return to it outside the traditional Church. The Bible Church movement with its insistence on "scripture only" is an example, as is also the "charismatic" movement.

[5] W. Windelband, *A History of Philosophy* (New York, 1901), p. 319. This book, which has been reproduced in a new printing by the publisher, provides a lucid and cogent description of how Western theology was shaped by pagan Greek philosophy.

[6] Georges Florovsky, *Creation and Redemption*. Vol. Three in Collected Works (Belmont, MA, 1972), p. 27.

[7] "Renaissance," meaning "rebirth," refers to the rediscovery and adoption of the classic Greek pagan culture. This produced "humanism," the philosophical doctrine that glorifies man as the center of things and the arbiter of his own destiny. It was the philosophy of the Renaissance and is the prevailing philosophy in our culture today, especially our public schools. It is the dominant philosophy among our intellectuals, some of whom have published several editions of a "Humanist Manifesto." They state, for example, "No diety will save us, we must save ourselves. Promises of immortal salvation or fear of eternal damnation are both illusory and harmful." The gospel and humanism are irreconcilable.

[8] Because the rational methods of pagan philosophy cannot accommodate the *mystery* of the gospel, discussions that fall outside those methods are in the West often labeled, somewhat pejoratively, "mystical," and those who engage in them "mystics." But this is a false dichotomy, again traceable to Aristotelian influence. All theology is of necessity "mystical," and to the extent that it is not "mystical" it is not theology (using the word in its accurate sense of "knowledge of God"), but "philosophy of religion," which is a different matter. This is why theology based on liturgy – worship – is the most valid. (See Note 7, Chapter 10.)

[9] One of the most insidious of modern secular ideas being thrust upon the Church is the doctrine of "progress." I shall never forget one Sunday morning being cornered in the narthex of a famous church in New York City by an eminent scientist. There was a theological brouhaha going on behind the scenes and he wanted to set me right. For almost an hour he patiently explained to me the entire problem as he saw it, which was that while science had "progressed" by leaps and bounds over the centuries, theology had stood still for a couple of milleniums and it was time to update it. He undoubtedly

knew his science, for he was a Nobel laureate, but he knew little about the gospel of love, obedience and sacrifice.

[10]George Cronk, *The Message of the Bible* (Crestwood, N.Y., 1982), p.123.

[11]In these latter days there has grown up the notion that interpretation of scripture is an individual matter because of the "priesthood of all believers" (1 Peter 2. 9). The undivided Church, of which we have been writing, did indeed believe in such a priesthood. One of the greatest of the Church Fathers, Irenaios of Lyons, who lived before A.D. 200, wrote, " . . . all the disciples of the Lord are Levites and priests." At the same time, however, the Church maintained a parallel tradition of the special authority of an ordained priesthood in line of succession from the Apostles (by laying on of hands) to perform the sacraments and to be responsible for transmitting the faith intact, Individualism was seen as destructive of the unity Christ prayed for.

Chapter Twelve

OFFERINGS AND
WARNINGS

Ask almost anyone what an "offering" is, and he will tell you it's when they pass the collection plate in Church. What we put in the collection plate, however, is almost the least of our offerings. This is such a large subject that we only touch on it here, but it has much to do with love and obedience.

Jesus' entire life was an offering to the Father on our behalf; and, being on our behalf, it was an offering also to us. We can accept or reject it. He gave it in obedience to the Father and in utter love for the Father and for us (Ephesians 5.2; Hebrews 10.10; etc.). Thus if we reject it (saying, as some do, "I don't need that Jesus stuff; I can get along without it . . . "), we reject love, the very thing we most want.

What should be our response to so great a gift as this?

Simply to do as Jesus did. In fact, he commanded, "that you love one another as [in the same way that, in that same degree to which] I have loved you" (John 15.12). And so we do, when as Christians we are *being the Church* Christ means us to be.

What Christ means for his Church is for there to be in it a great mutuality of love, of compassion and kindness, of lowliness, meekness and patience toward one another, and much forbearing and forgiving of one another (Colossians 3.12,13). This is the Grand Co-inherence we spoke of in Chapter 9. Yet it is not just we "members" of the Church who are involved, but Christ himself, for he said, " . . . as you did it to one of the least of these my brethren, you did it to me" (Matthew 25.40).

Christ, then, endorses the good we do toward one another

in his Church. It would be nice to think that this makes everything sweetness and light. Unfortunately, the "doing" Christ speaks of refers not just to the good but *to the evil.* So, if we deal *unlov-ingly* with our Christian neighbor, *that also are we doing to Christ,* for Christ is in our neighbor.

All this that we do with respect to one another (and thereby to Christ) *represents our offerings* in the Church. This is already far beyond the matter of the collection plate, but it goes farther yet.

It extends to bearing one another's burdens, and suffering. Saint Paul wrote, "Bear one another's burdens, and so fulfill the law [commands] of Christ." This is far more than just "helping each other out." It extends to actually sharing another's suffer-ing *through death itself.* We live one another's life; we die one another's death. And we can do this because, doing it *in Christ,* we need fear nothing of death, for Christ has conquered death; he said, "Greater love has no man than this, that a man lay down his life for his friends"(John 15.13). *Love is stronger than death.*

I remember reading as a teenager a news item that has re-mained with me ever since. It told of a man and his wife who were crossing a railroad track. Suddenly, just as a train was com-ing, she caught her heel in the track. She couldn't get it loose, and the shoe was buckled on so she couldn't get out of it. He could easily have jumped aside. Instead, he caught her and held her, and they died together. I am certain that into all eternity he was glad that he did, for he acted not like Adam, who be-trayed his wife, but like the man God means all men to be. Also, he acted as Christ did for his Church, giving up his life for it (Ephesians 5.25).

Most of us will never have the opportunity for so dramatic a choice. Ours is perhaps a harder way. For the sake of our neighbor (spouse, child – those nearest us) *we have to die daily to self.* Death once is not so bad. Death every hour is continual crucifixion, but *joy in Christ.* This is the paradox of our faith, of our life in Christ.

This is the essence of the Christian life: that we cannot sit back and muse and speculate and enjoy. We must act, and action means prayer, and perhaps suffering in silence when we can do nothing else. This is set forth by Paul in 1 Corinthians 12, in which he likens the body of the Church to the physical body. He writes, "If one member suffers, all suffer together . . ." (1 Corinthians 12.26), and then adds, " . . . if one member is honored, all rejoice together." The suffering of all makes the suffering of the one endurable. The rejoicing of all honors the one all the more. This is the Way of Life, of obedience in love, and it is glorious.

If it is so glorious, then why is it not instantly embraced by everyone? For one thing, people desire one side of the coin but not the other – the glory but not the suffering. What may give them greater pause, however, is fear that their offering may be rejected.

Let us take an almost mundane example. The ladies of the church are having a bake sale. There is Mrs. Cooke, who is proud of her baking and also an excessively sensitive person – a defective Christian, as are we all. She brings her best effort. The lady in charge says, "Oh dear. That's the third cake just like that, and they never do sell. Let's just put it here in the closet, and then you can take it home if we don't need it!" Could not the lady in charge have found *some* way to accept the offering? There is no keener hurt than to have one's offering rejected; for if we have offered in love, giving of ourselves, we feel that God himself (the whole universe – all that matters) has rejected *us*. The result of an offering's being rejected may even be murder, as we know from the story of Cain and Abel, which has profound significance for us. Love also is an offering, and fear of its rejection is one reason why so little love is offered. For the Christian, acceptance of offerings is just as important as giving them. Fortunately, *the Father never rejects our offerings,* if truly they are offered *to him in and through his Son, Jesus Christ, in whose hands he has put all things* (Ephesians 1.22). We, on the other hand, do reject Jesus' offering to us, and for this he suffers, saying nothing. We too must learn to suffer, bearing the rejection of our offerings by our fellow men (though without pride that the offerings are of any worth), that we may be like Christ.

That brings us to a most important point concerning *Church* and *offerings.* We have spoken in this book of the "traditional Church," of Protestant, of Catholic, of Orthodoxy, etc. There are obviously many formal divisions in the Church. Yet Jesus prayed that we may be *one,* and we saw that the nature of that unity is one of love and obedience. We need to remember that Jesus desires to *have us* more even than we desire to have him, or to have one another. His prayer for our unity is therefore as compelling a command as any he uttered. And since he lives in all eternity, he is assuredly praying that prayer even now. What are we to do about it?

A contrived "ecumenism" will not work, nor will the obliteration of differences in a sort of planned vagueness, a deceitful syncretism. In Matthew 18, the chapter containing one of the two mentions of "Church" in the gospel, we find a clue to what we are to do. The chapter begins with the disciples asking who is greatest in the kingdom (Church), and Jesus tells them that whoever humbles himself like a little child is greatest. (vv. 3,4) The rest of the chapter, including the entire context of the mention of "Church," concerns forgiveness. That, then is to be *our offering to God on behalf of our separated Christian brothers and sisters;* humility (our *self*-crucifixion) and our prayers of forgiveness for their errors, whatever they may be (God knows them; we cannot be certain of them), and *for our own.*

Even so, that makes it sound too *easy.* Our temptation is to pray, "I thank thee, Father, that I am not as my errant brother." But that is the Pharisee's prayer. It does not justify us before God. Our prayer must be that of the publican, "God, be merciful to me a sinner" (Luke 18.13). That means *every denomination must so pray.*

Still, it is hard for us to see the radical importance of this. The story of Cain and Abel, however, can teach us. The story in Genesis 4 is that Abel, "a keeper of sheep," brought to God an offering of the "firstlings of his flock," and God accepted it. Cain, a "tiller of the ground," brought an offering of his crops, and God rejected it. We have seen what rejection of an offering does to a person; it caused Cain to murder Abel. I have personally seen and heard, more often than I care to remember, Christians in their thoughts and hearts *murdering* other denominations that they found offensive, uttering *every* sort of calumny against them.

Could that be because they fear their brother's offering may be acceptable to God and their own not? God said to Cain, "If you do well, will you not be accepted" (Genesis 4.7)? What have we to fear? *We fear only because we do not love,* for "perfect love casts out fears, " as we saw in Chapter 7. Suppose if instead of murdering Abel, Cain had said to God, "Because I have offered of the fruit of the ground, you do not accept my offering, but what I have offered is food for my brother's cattle that they might have 'fat portions' [Genesis 4.4] such as you desire. Let my offering be one therefore that makes my brother's acceptable to you, and be merciful unto me, a sinner whose offering is not acceptable." According to Jesus, Cain's offering, like that of the publican, given in humility, would then be acceptable. To make offerings of prayer for one another, to suffer for one another and to ask God's forgiveness on behalf of one another, to live one another's life, to die one another's death – *that* is Church and the unity of it that Jesus prayed the Father we might have.

With respect to our brothers in Christ, of whatever division of Christendom they may be, *we are to be God's obedient servants, not his self-appointed deputies, usurping his power of judgment.* And if we do take upon ourselves the role of judge? Then we make *ourselves* God, and God will judge *us.* What an embarrassment if, when we come before the judgment of Christ, we hear him say, "You are not accepted on your merits but because this separated brother, whom you despised, has interceded for you."[1]

The unity of love among Christians does not mean "open communion" for all. Love is of a sterner quality than to permit the Eucharist to be approached casually. Baptism is a prerequisite. Preparation, discernment and understanding are essential, and Church authorities quite properly require assurance and verification.

Then is Christian unity possible? Jesus said, ". . . with God all things are possible" (Matthew 19.26; also Mark 10.27 and 14.36). Let us unite our prayer for unity with Christ's, then God will himself bring it about.

Jesus' Commands to His Churches

If we serve the Church in love, it must be in obedience. But did Jesus leave any specific commands concerning his Church? He did, and they are among the most neglected of all his commands.

They are found in the second and third chapters of Revelation. Jesus himself is instructing seven congregations of his Church. (We should bear in mind that although it is not yet 70 years since Jesus' death, many of the prayers and liturgical formulas that endure even today, together with a strong sacramental life in the Church, are already well established.) The seven congregations are clearly typical of *all* congregations *then* and *now.* The commands are therefore meant to be warnings to us and to all churches in all times.

* * * * *

The first message is addressed to the Church at Ephesos, where Paul worked for three years and where, according to tradition, John, the beloved disciple, ended his earthly labors. Jesus commends them for their work, toil and patient endurance. Moreover, he praises them "because you cannot bear evil men." This should bring us up short. A deep hatred of evil was characteristic of the early Church. Is it so today? Or do we, rather, fail to condemn evil, and in a mistaken charity condone it, insisting that there are no "evil men" but only "misguided" ones? This is a misapplication of "judge not lest ye be judged." It is a return to the pagan "live and let live" that has been revived by modern "psychology." Jesus condemns it.

Then comes Jesus' most serious accusation: " . . . you have abandoned the love you had at first." What was that? It was the first enthusiastic, loving and obedient devotion of the Church to her Lord. The passage parallels Jeremiah 2.2: "I remember the devotion of your youth, your love as a bride . . . " The eager raptures of our first love – all the mutualities of the Grand Coinherence that we spoke of – must become permanent. Jesus therefore commands, " . . . repent and do the works you did at first" (Revelation 2.5). Our churches today must hear and observe this.

If the Ephesians disobey, God will remove their "lampstand." This has happened. Once a glorious city of the Roman Empire, Ephesos is today a squalid Mohammedan village with not a Christian in sight. Should we not consider the possibility that something like this could happen to our cities and churches?

Jesus commends the Ephesians for hating the works of the Nicolaitans, "which I also hate." The Nicolaitans were followers of Nicholas, an apostle from Antioch, who indulged in extreme sensuality. They taught that in order to master sensuality one should know the whole range of it by experience! They were a Gnostic sect with a peculiar twist to their thought. While the Gnostics generally held that matter was evil, the Nicolaitans held that lustful practices are harmless because they do not affect the spirit, which alone is important. The Nicolaitans are at large in our secular culture today, and they are getting into some of our churches. There are indeed no new heresies.

But Jesus says to the Ephesians, and to us, "To him who conquers I will grant to eat of the tree of life, which is in the paradise of God" (Revelation 2.7). We recall that man's sin was the occasion for his being driven from paradise (Eden), " . . . lest he put forth his hand and take also of the tree of life, and eat, and live forever . . . " (Genesis 3.22,23). Now we are restored to life with God in paradise – *if we conquer.*

* * * * *

The command to the Church at Smyrna involves both a prophecy and an encouragement, as revelant now as it was then. Jesus said, "Do not fear what you are about to suffer . . . Be faithful unto death . . ." (Revelation 2.10).

They were about to suffer persecution. The first bishop of Smyrna was Polycarp, one of the great Apostolic fathers, who knew John personally, as well as many others of Jesus' immediate disciples. About A.D. 155, when he was a very old man, there was a pagan festival in the stadium at Smyrna for which eleven Christians had been brought to be fed to lions. At the end, the crowd demanded Polycarp. A pyre was constructed and Polycarp was burned to death on it. He and his fellow martyrs at Smyrna received the fulfillment of Jesus' promise, "Be faithful unto death, and I will give you the crown of life"(Revelation 2.10). The "crown" here is not the garland of victory , as in the Olympic games, but an emblem of royalty, a sign of lordship over life itself!

Martyrdoms are again today the lot of Christians. Innumerably more have died for the faith in this century in the Soviet Union and in Communist China than ever were martyred under the Roman Empire. We are being propagandized today that there is "freedom of religion" under Communism. But let a Communist try to convert to Christianity, and he will be martyred. No Christian alive today can be certain he will *not* become a martyr to his faith. Christ's promise of the "crown" is to us all.

* * * * *

In his message to the Church at Pergamum (Pergamos) Jesus tells them he knows all about their city. It is "where Satan's throne is" (Revelation 2.13). It is "where Satan dwells." This is hardly suprising. Pergamum was an opulent place, a crossroads of the world with three rivers watering lush groves that were the site of licentious pagan rites. (One thinks of Central Park in New York City, and how many other parks in other cities, and the hidden – more or less – "rites" that go on there.) Not surprisingly, there were Nicolaitans in the Church here also, advocating sensuality. Jesus commands them, "Repent then" (Revelation 2.16). If they do not, then Jesus says, "I will come to you soon and war against them with the sword of my mouth."

God is not permissive. He conducts warfare. He is not a

"grandfather in heaven" raining benevolence on all, but an exacting father who sets the standard for his children. We feel the warfare in our conscience, for his very words accuse us (and he will not repent his words, for they are eternal – they are the "sword of his mouth"); and if *we* do not repent we will suffer damage both inwardly and outwardly. The Church must heed conscience and submit to the discipline of God.

* * * * *

The Church at Thyatira, some 60 miles northeast of Smyrna, Jesus commends for their love, faith, service and patient endurance. He commands them to hold fast to those good things that they have. He rebukes them, however, for the woman "Jezebel," who calls herself a prophetess and is teaching the young men immorality. She apparently also leads a cult that seeks the "deep things of Satan." Her name obviously stands for the villainous wife of King Ahab in 1 and 2 Kings, and this tells us the kind of person she is and what God thinks of her. Jesus says he will throw her on a sickbed and those who commit adultery with her will face big trouble. Then he adds, " . . . *and I will strike her children dead*" (Revelation 2.23).

This is rough stuff. God means business. It's *us* against *him* (if we will it to be so), and in the showdown we, not God, are broken and die – not because *he* so wills it, but because *we* will have it so. No wonder we are to "fear Him," as we saw in Chapter 7.

Does this really cause us great concern today? Do we really purge our churches of unrepentant offenders? Or do we consider ourselves too "modern," or "liberal," or "emancipated" for that sort of thing? It is not easy to obey Christ. Recently a church in Oklahoma expelled an errant and unrepentant member, and she sued the Church and was awarded $400,000 in the secular courts.[2] Government today is obedient to pagan standards, not God's. Yet Jesus said, " . . . all the churches shall know that I am he who searches mind and heart, and I will give to each of you as your works deserve" (Revelation 2.23).

* * * * *

Except for the one to the Church in Laodicea, Jesus' rebuke to the Church in Sardis is the most stinging of all. It should be posted in large letters in every church in America, so that all can see it every Sunday. Jesus said, "I know your works; you have the name of being alive, *and you are dead*" (Revelation 3.1).

What are the "works" that give Sardis the "name" of being alive when in fact dead? Probably the same as those that give so many churches the "name" of being "alive"today: social functions, clubs,sewing circles, arts and crafts, bazaars, sports teams, recreational events. I remember very vividly sitting in a committee meeting in one of the largest and most prestigious churches in the United States and saying, "Do you people realize, that in this church you can get courses in a dozen arts and crafts, including 'How to Make After Five Hats', but absolutely nothing on how to study the Bible and learn about Jesus Christ?" This was considered very inappropriate and I was nearly thrown out of the meeting.

First comes obedience to Christ. Other activities of the church community are secondary. The command to the Church at Sardis is a command to us all: "Awake, and strengthen what remains and is on the point of death . . . "(Revelation 3.2). What is it that remains? Simply those elements of the Way of Life that we have been discussing. Of them Jesus says, "Remember then what you received and heard; keep that and repent" (v. 3). If they will not awake, Jesus says, "I will come like a thief, and you will not know at what hour I will come upon you." And what does a thief do? He takes away what we most value, and puts us out of business.

*   *   *   *   *

Not every Church was rebuked. Jesus commanded the Church in Philadelphia, " . . . hold fast what you have, so no one may seize your crown" (Revelation 3.11). His message is pure poetry of love and promise of glory:

He who conquers, I will make him a pillar in the temple of my God; never shall he go out of it, and I will write on him the name of my God, and the name of the city of my God, the New Jerusalem which comes down from my God, out of heaven, and my own new name (Revelation 3.12,13).

If by a miracle of God's grace our own Church here today should happen to be like that in Philadelphia, then let us by all means redouble our concentration on the command to "hold fast," for we will be under continuous assault by Satan to make us depart from the commands and love of Jesus.

* * * * *

Jesus' most blistering rebuke is reserved for the Church in Laodicea. Their fault is, " . . . you are neither cold nor hot." Jesus says then, "So, because you are lukewarm, and neither cold nor hot, I will spew you out of my mouth."(Revelation 3.16).

Actually, the Greek word is stronger than "spew." It means: *vomit.* So now we know what happens to lukewarm Christians. They become God's vomit. This goes back to Jesus' saying to his disciples, "You are the salt of the earth . . . " (Matthew 5.13). But he adds that if it has become insipid, lost its "saltness" (become "lukewarm"), it is no longer good for anything except to be thrown out and "trodden under foot by men." Vomited by God, trampled by men. Such is to be our fate if we are tepid toward God.

Do you know any congregations like that? Or perhaps one should ask; how many do you know that are *not* like that? Laodicea is most churches today. But consider the commands: to *love God* with all our being; to love our neighbor *as if he were ourselves;* to enter pain, suffering, sorrow and even death with Jesus for his sake and our neighbor's; to evangelize the whole world, starting with those around us, including also the Jews. If we do not do these things we should not be surprised that God vomits us out of his mouth, until we repent.

"Draw near to God," says James, "and he will draw near to you" (James 4.8). But when we get near we learn the reality that "our God is a consuming *fire*" (Hebrews 12.29). He wants to burn up our egos and substitute himself in their place, *We are the "gold refined by fire"* that Jesus wants the Laodiceans (us) to buy from him that they (we) may be truly rich. (Revelation 3.18). We "buy"it through our submission to chastening, which is not for punishment but for discipline, purification and humility.

What then? Let us keep with us always what Jesus says to us, the Laodiceans:

> Behold, I stand at the door and knock; if any one hears my voice and opens the door, I will come to him and eat with him, and he with me. He who conqueres, I will grant him to sit with me *on my throne* as I myself conquered and sat down with my Father on his throne. He who has an ear, let him hear what the Spirit says to the churches (Revelation 3.20-22).

* * * * *

Jesus knocks, continually seeking those who will love and obey him. He gave himself, and continues to give himself, *for us*. Can we respond witrh anything less than love and total obedience? What can we desire more than to be his friend, to "sit on his throne," and through him receive everything we ask for? Our desires are not too great, but too pitifully small, compared to what Jesus wants to give us. He said:

> My command is this: Love each other as I have loved you. Greater love has no one than this, that one lay down his life for his friends. You are my friends if you do what I command. I no longer call you servants, because a servant does not know his master's business. Instead, I have called you friends, for everything that I learned from my Father I have made known to you. You did not choose me, but I chose

you to go and bear fruit – fruit that will last. Then the Father will give you whatever you ask in my name. This is my command: Love each other (John 15.12-17).[3]

Notes

[1] Micheal Bourdeaux, an Anglican priest and founder of Keston College in England, an institute for the study of religion in Communist countries, writes in *Risen Indeed: Lessons in Faith from the USSR* how the persecuted churches in the Soviet Union are truly one in love, caring and praying for each other as Christ commanded. Overt persecution of the churches in the United States is at hand, and even now under way. Can we not also find the humility to love and pray for one another as Christ commanded us?

[2] Marian Guinn *vs.* The Church of Christ of Collinsville, Oklahoma, District Court in and for Tulsa County, State of Oklahoma. The court decision is being appealed and is therefore not yet precedent for similar cases. There are in the United States some 2,000 cases currently pending in the same secular courts against Christian churches and their clergy. These can be expected to increase as government moves with a vengeance against Christianity.

[3] *The New International Version* (Grand Rapids, 1978).